Emergent Teaching

A Path of Creativity, Significance, and Transformation

Sam Crowell and David Reid-Marr

ROWMAN & LITTLEFIELD EDUCATION
A division of
ROWMAN & LITTLEFIELD PUBLISHERS, INC.
Lanham • New York • Toronto • Plymouth, UK

Published by Rowman & Littlefield Education
A division of Rowman & Littlefield Publishers, Inc.
A wholly owned subsidary of The Rowman & Littlefield Publishing Group, Inc.
4501 Forbes Boulevard, Suite 200, Lanham, Maryland 20706
www.rowman.com

10 Thornbury Road, Plymouth PL6 7PP, United Kingdom

British Library Cataloguing in Publication Information Available

Library of Congress Cataloging-in-Publication Data Available

ISBN 978-1-4758-0254-2 (cloth : alk. paper) — ISBN 978-1-4758-0255-9 (pbk. : alk. paper) —
ISBN 978-1-4758-0256-6 (electronic)

©™ The paper used in this publication meets the minimum requirements of American
National Standard for Information Sciences Permanence of Paper for Printed Library
Materials, ANSI/NISO Z39.48-1992.

Printed in the United States of America

We dedicate this book to our students who taught and inspired us, and paved a way for our thinking. We dedicate it also to the new breed of educators who fearlessly open their minds and hearts to the possibilities of an emergent, transforming education.

Sam:
To my dad. And to Lily.

David:
For my parents: Tom, Lyn, Mike, and Marjorie

Contents

Preface

This book is a narrative inquiry into the concept of *emergence* as it is experienced within the context of teaching. Emergence is an essential part of the newer sciences of complexity and chaos. And these fields of inquiry are contained within the larger, more general umbrella of open systems theory.

The ideas expressed here are a natural outcome of our extended discourse and ongoing conversations. From these have come collaboratively taught courses, presentations, talks, one article, and an invited chapter about our work (in Ashton and Denton, 2006). But at the heart of these conversations has been an elaboration of our stories and experiences.

At some point we realized that our stories were, at least metaphorically, illustrations of the principles of emergence. We began to explore the subtleties and nuances of our experience as an inquiry into what these principles actually mean and how they can be applied to the teaching process. This opened up a new understanding of complexity and both the practical and philosophical implications.

The concept of emergence has similarities to Piaget's use of autopoiesis and self-organization and is related to Prigogine's research in thermodynamics. However emergence cannot be fully understood outside the context of complexity and chaos theory. These areas of scientific inquiry are still in their infancy and they remain highly abstract and mathematical. Yet they have also captured the imagination of researchers in fields other than physics and mathematics.

Because the language of complexity, chaos, and emergence is highly metaphorical they elicit assumptions that are not necessarily consistent with theoretical constructs or are overly simplistic when translated into applied situations. Nevertheless, we believe the science-based particulars as well as the metaphor of emergence can be used to understand transformational processes that occur in everyday life.

The sciences of complexity, chaos, and cognitive constructive theory do share some common assumptions that can be applied to a deeper understanding of holistic relationships, dynamical change, and emerging patterns of organization (see Fleener et al., 2005, p. 9). We find these ideas particularly relevant to teaching and to the understanding of transformational shifts that occur in our own lives and in the lives of our students.

These ideas especially inform the areas of creativity, process-oriented activity, and dynamics of community. Finally, we see in the metaphorical unpacking of emergence a resonance with wisdom traditions that have informed human history for millennia and remain with us as guides and reminders of our natural wisdom.

So we are not setting out to create yet another educational theory or to construct a model based on an abstract synthesis from these sciences. Rather, the two of us see this book as a form of narrative inquiry—an exploration if you will—of abstract concepts and ideas as we have come to understand them in our teaching.

What interests us most is how emergence can be used to cultivate the heart and art of teaching. How can we use a more contextual perspective to rethink what it means to teach and learn? While this book comes from the vantage point of our own technical understanding of emergence, the emphasis is on the narrative of our experience: the life-world of the teacher.

While metaphorical analysis is more philosophical than technical, in its applied form it emphasizes implications and applications. Also, as part of the larger theoretical constructs of complexity and chaos theories, emergence leads to a reconsideration of some of the fundamental assumptions in education. It provides one more anomaly that forces us to question the efficacy of the modernist paradigm and its usefulness for the issues we face in the era in which we live.

The themes of the book are particularly relevant to discussions that deal with teaching the whole person, new understandings of process, project-based learning, transformative learning, incorporating story and narrative, and building community in the classroom. The content also addresses the holistic, embodied nature of the learning process and the importance of the arts in constructing meaning. Since these topics are typically part of most methods courses they can be easily adapted to the coursework of preservice teachers.

The content is organized around stories and illustrations of what we are calling emergent teaching. A more linear presentation of the ideas of emergent teaching is provided in the last chapter as well as a question-and-answer section related to the needs and concerns of teachers.

This book is also relevant for those courses in curriculum studies and foundations that explore the contemporary intellectual landscape. Our view of emergence has its roots in constructive postmodernist thought where creative potential is emphasized rather than deconstructed relativism. While we question the prevailing assumptions about teaching and learning, we also offer a realistic and tangible alternative that can be applied to the everyday context of the classroom.

Individually, the authors' personal histories situate the content and focus of this book. We share our histories because we feel they may inform the reading of the book and the nuanced themes contained in it.

Sam was trained in social foundations at the University of Virginia. His dissertation was a philosophical analysis of quantum mechanics, holography, and systems theory in terms of their implications for education and for a new cultural mythology. He has experience in both elementary and high school settings, has served as university director and coordinator of elementary teacher training programs, and is the founder of a graduate degree program in holistic and integrative education.

His academic focus throughout his career has been in the area of applied philosophy that has included translating the "new sciences" into educational understandings, interpreting neuroscience research for classroom practice, and applying holistic perspectives and transformative approaches to teaching and learning. As a founding member of the Spirituality and Education network, Sam has infused contemplative approaches into much of his teaching. He has advocated for an inspirited education and a responsive connection to learning. Sam recently received university recognition for his outstanding teaching.

David obtained his MFA in art at the Royal College of Art in London and has remained a practicing artist throughout his adult life. In addition, he was trained and ordained as a Zen monk and served as such for many years until he felt he needed to enter the everyday world and see how Zen practice worked there. Teaching is informed by his life as an artist; this includes sculpture, drawing, performance, and site-specific work.

David teaches visual arts at the Idyllwild Arts Academy, a unique and highly regarded arts high school, and is an adjunct professor at California State University, San Bernardino. Art, and the creative insight that inspires it, doesn't have the same limitations as purely intellectual pursuits; it allows for the emotional and creative life of the students to unfold, and it is no exaggeration to say that this process is inclusive of all sensibilities and abilities.

Emergent teaching occurs within a particular kind of democratic space that Osberg (2010) explains makes room for paradox. She raises the essential question that persists in this kind of education, "Where is the 'democratic space,' with paradox at its heart, that allow people to engage with . . . the possibility of the impossible" (p. 164). It is our hope that this book conveys the spirit of this challenge and readers will be both inspired and informed to teach in a new way.

Acknowledgments

This book has evolved over a number of years with many twists and turns. It could not have been written without the help and support of a lot of people. First, we want to recognize our students who have given us the gift of their inspiration, insights, and authenticity. This book is theirs. Our friend and colleague, Dr. Robert London, is part of every page. May you fly with the eagles, Bob.

We are also thankful for our many friends at the International Conference for Holistic Education and for the opportunity to present our ideas in their early stages of development. This group of holistic educators inspired us in so many ways. We also want to acknowledge the support of our institutions, California State University, San Bernardino, and the Idyllwild Arts Academy. They accepted us as mavericks and have let us be who we are.

Our many conversations were highlighted by the food and atmosphere at Café Aroma. Our discussions on creativity always included our admiration of Frank Ferro and the way he creates laughter, enjoyment, and community for others. And keeping us honest with his questions and support is Dr. Hubert Halkin.

Sam: My family has always been there with support and encouragement. Without Debbie, Chesley, Lily, and Bob in my life, this book would have little meaning for me. Thanks go to Bill Doll for all his gracious support and mentorship; to Renate and Geoffrey Caine who have meant so much to me over the years; to Jason Siff for his friendship and wisdom; to Mirian Villela for her kindness and the enduring work she does for the International Earth Charter; and to my morning coffee buddies who make me laugh and keep me grounded—Lou, Vic, Connor, Pete, and Frank. This book will always be a tribute to the memory of my father and all he has meant to me.

David: Thank you to Jennifer and our children: May, Adam, Vesper, and Jovielle, and the little ones Rasalas and Serena. You have taught me so much about play, love, and learning. To my brave siblings Godfrey, Carole, and Margaret. To William Turnbull for introducing me to the liberating world of contemporary art. To Maezumi Roshi for his Zen teaching of anything and everything, and Steve Hudson for sharing his beautiful, irrepressible life.

Introduction

Our educational system is in deep trouble. The core of the problem is that learning has become about accumulating information for its own sake. But information in itself, without context, is meaningless, sterile, lifeless. It has no relationship to our deepest concerns. Testing and accountability systems focus only on the display of knowledge or the instrumental demonstration of skills isolated from real problems or genuine inquiry. External performance is too often unrelated to students' inner world where they long for meaning, purpose, and significance.

Most of what research says about learning disputes these kinds of practices, yet the system continues with pacing guides, fragmentation of subject matter, and no real attempt to connect to the life-worlds of students. In the 1960s there was a plea for relevance. In the 1980s research pointed us toward meaning-centered curricula.

Now as we are well into the twenty-first century, we are calling for a more responsive learning, where knowledge becomes connected to who we are as human beings—not just intellectual capacities but our capacity for altruistic concern, selfless service, collaborative action, and creative wisdom. These characteristics are contained in what we call *emergent teaching*.

EMERGENT CURRICULUM AND EMERGENT TEACHING

There is a difference between emergent curriculum and what we refer to as emergent teaching. Most of the literature on emergent curriculum is focused on preschool and early childhood programs. These curricula are represented as complex projects carried out over an extended period of time. The Reggio Emilia approach is a very good example.

The Reggio Emilia curriculum is built upon student interests and ideas, in a purposeful, aesthetic learning environment and guided by an experiential perspective of learning. This very successful early learning approach and other similar models are rarely continued once children enter the K-12 system. In fact, it is not until one reaches the doctoral or MFA level that this kind of learning reappears. The two of us remember the joy and rigor of these learning experiences and how transformational this kind of instruction became in our overall development.

The emphasis of this book, however, is on *emergent teaching*. Rather than offer a curricular approach that is unlikely to be accepted in the present context of No Child Left Behind and the myopic preoccupation with test scores, we want to address those everyday moments where opportunities for personal and authentic encounters with students exist.

We encourage teachers to take advantage of occasions as they present themselves, not necessarily as planned and pre-scripted events but as a response to what arises naturally. This may be with a single student or with a whole class, but it almost always presents itself as something other than a purely cognitive response. Sometimes entire assignments and projects can be built into the existing curriculum. Often they are fleeting moments of possibility and from these moments a conversation is begun in which we discover something important about ourselves and our world.

As teachers, we are not trained in spontaneity and improvisation; ours is primarily a profession of control, of planning. When teaching becomes a form of structured improvisation, however, we need new *understandings* and *perceptions* to guide us. *Practices* can be developed that encourage more personal and creative responses. We can cultivate *dispositions* that lead to greater awareness and presence in the classroom. And yes, there are ways to transcend the current curricula that can be applied to any grade level or subject matter, with grade level teams, middle school learning communities, high school departments, or university programs.

Our main purpose in this book is to share the stories of our experience in a way that embeds the *understandings, perceptions, practices, and dispositions* we have discovered in emergent teaching. Emergent teaching is a different way of perceiving our role as teachers. It includes engagement, playful discovery, deep inquiry, and creativity. When these qualities are present the space for emergence opens up.

ORGANIZATION OF THE BOOK

The first chapter introduces the reader to the concept of emergence and the use of stories and multithreaded tales. It sets the stage for a theoretical discussion. Chapter 2 uses the myth of Indra's Net to illustrate that the universe is inherently connected, relational, and dynamically changing. These ideas provide the foundation for emergence and emergent teaching. We present stories that illustrate how everyday teaching can be a vehicle for substantive, self-reflective inquiry and how such inquiry provides opportunities for transformation. The first two chapters provide an orientation for the other topics in the book.

It is in the midst of process that habitual patterns of learning and relating to the world and others are dissolved. Chapter 3 uses anecdotes to demonstrate the effectiveness of process learning, which requires open and adaptive systems. These include physical, emotional, and aesthetic environments that are malleable, where collaborative exchanges can take place, and that are rooted in experience. Emergent teaching is grounded in process.

Chapter 4 focuses on the concepts of nonlinearity, chaos, and complexity. Emergence requires a more meandering process that allows both the student and teacher to follow inquiry wherever it leads. This chapter explores nonlinearity through narratives that reflect the shifts that occur when meandering is practiced.

A focused but relaxed and playful state of mind has been supported by optimal performance research for decades. It is rarely applied to educational environments. In chapter 5, a connection is made between these qualities and emergence and, by implication, the creative process. Examples from the arts are used to illustrate these principles, and stories are provided that embed the processes and conditions required to make these ideas a reality.

Chapter 6 extends the previous discussion of emergent teaching to include more broadly the significance of creativity. The fact that we are biologically prone to creativity has significant implications for teaching and learning. This chapter seeks to go to the heart of what creativity means.

Chapter 7 introduces a discussion where ceremony and ritual become keys in the integration of learning and the building of community. The holistic nature of emergent teaching is emphasized here, and examples illustrate how context, process, and application can significantly enhance all learning.

Education is too often separated from an active engagement in the world. Chapter 8 presents learning as an ongoing journey of emancipation and service and shows how each can become natural outcomes of the curriculum.

When a teacher is in the midst of emergent teaching there is a point of ambiguity where outcomes are unknown, where imposed understandings are released, where autonomy and meaning become paramount, and where multiple possibilities are waiting to unfold. Chapter 9 offers an alternative understanding of the nature of curriculum and a holistic perspective in which learning engages the whole person.

The format of this book is built around multithreaded tales that are used to explore important concepts, ideas, and understandings around emergence. Chapter 10 provides a more direct and linear presentation of ways to implement emergent teaching in classrooms. It gives explicit suggestions about the classroom environment, community building, assignments, management, and staff development. Finally, it encourages teachers to develop and share their own stories of emergent teaching and the transformative impact it has on students' lives.

Chapter One

What Is Emergent Teaching?

Anyone who has spent time in the classroom has experienced those un-planned and unexpected moments throughout the day that lead to both head-aches and joy, puzzlement and opportunity. In the classroom, uncertainty prevails; complexity is a constant. As teachers, we are always creatively adapting to the environment, no matter how well-planned, organized, or structured the class may be.

Creative adaptation is even more apparent in classrooms where students are engaged and involved in their own learning, where they are given choices, and where learning is facilitated rather than delivered. To be successful in creative adaptation, there is a subtle perceptual shift that accepts the fact that we are *part of* the environment, *within* it, *moving dynamically* with it.

These teachers realize they can influence but not control what is happening. And this is a beautiful thing! The many surprises and opportunities that come about naturally from this kind of openness and acceptance make teaching one of the most rewarding and satisfying professions one can choose.

What occurs in these moments of spontaneity is never the same. Certain things can be anticipated, but the unique nature of each individual student and class is far from predictable. If these moments are given the space to unfold, the results are often transformative. It may or may not have anything to do with the curriculum, but we glimpse what education can be when it is authentic—that discovery of personal significance and a connected, resonate sense of belonging. We call this emergent teaching.

WHAT IS EMERGENCE?

The concept of emergence is a relatively recent idea in science. It is tied to the study of open and dynamic systems that are constantly interacting with their environment—changing, adapting, and evolving. The "emergent" system continuously exchanges energy and information with its surroundings, thus influencing even as it, too, is influenced.

What is interesting is that the larger system, or whole, is always being defined and redefined by the complex interactions, adaptations, and decisions being made. This actually has broad implications for teaching. But first let's look at the science that informs these ideas.

Johnson (2001) describes how emergent behavior responds "to the specific, and changing needs of the environment" (p. 20). It is a type of "bottom-up" intelligence where the whole and the parts are constantly changing themselves through continuous interaction and interplay. Knowledge is dynamically adaptive and reflexive, folding back onto and into the subject even as it extends outward onto and into the larger environment.

Does this suggest subjectivism? Yes, but not in the way we usually think of subjectivity. For example, slime molds and ant colonies are particular cases of emergence where "macrointelligence and adaptability derive from local knowledge" (p. 77), yet emergence in these systems is based on the reflexive processes of the micro and macro exchanges of information. This happens throughout nature and is part of a larger understanding of the inherent creativity of the universe.

Ilya Prigogine (1984), a Nobel laureate in chemistry, was one of the early pioneers to identify complex, self-organizing systems where "individual action or each local intervention has a collective aspect that can result in quite unanticipated global changes" (p. 203). This means that the seemingly insignificant event can influence the entire system in a way that cannot be predicted or anticipated.

Understanding self-organizing systems in terms of these kinds of patterns and processes involves a very different kind of science. Complex structures such as coastlines, forests, mountain chains, ice sheets, and star clusters cannot be examined or explained simply by cause-effect ideas about nature. Nor can learning.

The ideas, understandings, and assumptions embedded in the concept of emergent systems are in contrast to the conventional worldview that governs most of our institutional behavior. As the world becomes more complex, the linear descriptive models and practices will become less and less workable and less and less relevant.

Everyday observations reveal emergence to be present in many aspects of our experience. Nevertheless, emergence represents a fundamentally different way of understanding ourselves and nature. Rather than a machine view of the universe, where the parts are merely constitutive of the whole and may even be considered irrelevant, emergence suggests that each part is always reflecting as well as remaking the greater whole.

Instead of perceiving the "things" of nature to be self-contained and existing separately unto themselves, emergence describes a world of constant change and interaction, a world in which separation is an illusion. In contrast to the perception that interactive relationships can be predetermined and predefined, emergence invites us to see how all relationships are constantly defining themselves around the particular situation and context as it arises.

So the concept of emergence encourages us to rethink some of the most basic assumptions we have used to organize our views of reality. Not only is this significant scientifically, but it has important ramifications for the way we think about education.

EMERGENCE AND EDUCATION

When attention is turned to the human experience to understand what these new ideas mean for living life and thinking about learning, there is a need to be aware of the parts and the whole simultaneously. One cannot understand oneself without some understanding of context within the natural and social environment.

The classical model of seeing learning as merely information processing is inadequate as it completely ignores any reference to the internal states of the individual. However, recent cognitive research suggests otherwise; information is processed in order to create meaning about some aspect of experience. Meaning connects students to the world they inhabit and allows them to be active agents in that world. Meaning cannot be given to someone; it is part of the self-organizing process of the individual.

The fact that the ideas of emergence are part of new ways of thinking and understanding can be seen in some of the recent theoretical models in cognitive science and neuropsychology. Evan Thompson (2007) builds on the work of neuroscientist Francisco Varela and makes a strong case for what he calls embodied dynamicism or an enactive cognitive theory.

> Embodied dynamicism focuses on self-organizing dynamic systems rather than physical symbol systems but maintains in addition that cognitive processes emerge from the nonlinear and circular causality of continuous sensorimotor interactions involving the brain, body, and environment. (pp. 10–11)

This sounds extremely technical but is an important foundation for this book. The quotation by Thompson supports the idea that learners, as cognitive agents, both define and are defined by internal and external processes that are always in flux and are always adapting to one another. Therefore, emergence suggests a different view of cognition. Thompson defines cognition as "the exercise of skillful know-how in situated and embodied action" (p. 11). This is consistent with emergent teaching.

There are five important assumptions that Thompson develops (p. 13). The first is that *humans are autonomous agents who enact and engage in the world*. Learning, then, is tied to a sense of human agency and action. Thinking is organized in relation to one's lived experience.

The second point is that *the entire nervous system is involved in creating meaning and generating meaningful patterns of activity*. To not engage students in expressive and consolidating opportunities is to inhibit their natural propensities to learn.

Third, *cognition is situated, contextual, and active*. The individual couples with the environment in continuous patterns of perception and action. Therefore, subject matter is naturally integrative and to treat it as disembodied and self-contained is to create a picture of reality as fragmented and meaningless.

A fourth assumption is that *the world is mutually cocreated as a relational domain*. In other words, we "take in" the world even as we act upon it. Who one is and how one perceives the world matters.

And, fifth, *experience is central to any understanding of the mind*. Individuals simply cannot be separated from their experience. These assumptions are relevant to and descriptive of emergent teaching.

To understand learning as an emergent process, we must begin to rethink the comfortable linear models that pervade educational culture. Emergent teaching is one way to begin to apply these ideas in our classrooms, not in the abstract, but in real, concrete ways.

SITUATING EMERGENT TEACHING

Emergence is not a methodology or a pedagogical theory; it is simply a description of the behavior of complex adaptive systems. And we human beings fall into that category. We are living organisms, not machines. We are agents in the world searching for purpose and meaning in our lives.

A pedagogy developed from a technical mindset is bound to be misguided and ultimately unfruitful. This is not just a pedagogical statement but one that also applies to any situation in which fixed, linear models alone are used to manage and control open, adaptive, complex systems. Our current educational models will not work in contexts where complexity, creative chaos, and openness are required.

An organismic view of the universe is not new. It has ancient roots ι. both Eastern and Western cultures and in indigenous societies as well. What is new is the science behind these ideas and the contrasting paradigm this presents to the dominant mechanistic and reductionist worldview of our time.

Emergent teaching is not a repackaged romanticism, nor is it a newly constructed vocabulary for progressive education. But it is reminiscent of these traditions. Philosophically, emergence is much more aligned with what has been labeled constructive postmodernism (Griffin, 1995; Doll, 1993; Crowell, 2001) and espouses a radical contextualism and interconnectedness. It specifically uses and develops the language and questions of wholeness rather than reductionism.

All postmodernisms argue that many of the ideas that arose intellectually in the Enlightenment period can no longer be supported by either philosophical argument or twentieth-century science. Among these are the concepts of mechanism, reductionism, and dualism—concepts that describe nature and the universe as disconnected from experience, as isolated entities subject only to the external, causally determined world (Crowell, 1995).

These notions became embedded in modern science, which assumed that the material world in its observable form is complete unto itself. In education, for example, behaviorism does not address any internal processing, only external, observable behavior. For example, teachers create objectives that are determinative, observable, and measurable.

Throughout mainstream education goals such as learning to appreciate, to inspire, to grow, and to understand are deemed inappropriate as objectives unless they can written in measurable terms. This illustrates how a great deal of the human experience is not addressed or even taken into consideration as legitimate areas of discourse. Such is the influence of modernism. There is a falsity to this that intuitively for many teachers just doesn't make sense.

Walker Percy (1959), in his provocative midcentury poem, wrote that "the modern age began to come to an end when men discovered that they could no longer understand themselves by the theory professed by the age" (p. 25). And Berman (1981) notes that the progressive disenchantment of the last three hundred years has produced "a rigid distinction between observer and observed. There is not ecstatic merger with nature, but rather total separation from it. Subject and object are always seen in opposition to each other" (p. 16).

These kinds of social critiques are also evident within science itself. Toulmin (1982) suggested that new scientific understandings have toppled the foundations that created them. Science "has not yet discovered how to define itself in terms of what it is, but only in terms of what it has just-now-ceased-to-be" (p. 254).

Physicist Paul Davies (1983) in summarizing the discoveries of what he calls the "new sciences" concludes that it is like "turning three hundred years of science on its head" (p. 22). Emergence is part of these new understandings that radically reframe the scientific landscape.

Historically, both Ludwig von Bertalanffy, as the articulator of general systems theory, and Alfred North Whitehead, who developed process philosophy, were synthesizers of the more dynamic understandings of science being produced in the early twentieth century. Whitehead, in particular, had a major influence on what is loosely termed "constructive" postmodernism.

According to Cobb (2003), Whitehead emphasized the shift from substance thinking to event thinking. This view suggests that what we think of as concrete and real are actually dynamically changing events. Dewey was clearly influenced by these ideas. Although he never broke the hold that classical science had on him, his work on process, experience, art, and change did much to advance our understandings. In addition, Dewey's view of education as applied philosophy also served to tie education to these emerging concepts of dynamism and change.

In the current context, constructive postmodernism is more descriptive of an agenda perhaps than a philosophical tradition. It seeks to reconceptualize what new developments in science seem to suggest philosophically.

For example, if one samples the conceptual language generated during the last century of science you will find decidedly nonmodernist language: wholeness, connectedness, process, dynamism, subjective/objective complementarities, relatedness, nonseparate unities, indivisible continuities, nonsequential and randomized events, wholes within parts, self-similarity, emergent order, coevolving relationships, transformative change, becoming, event-filled phenomena, cooperative adaptation, community, and so on.

These terms represent significant anomalies from modernist descriptions of the universe. They represent a fundamentally different set of assumptions. It is this sense of wholeness, relatedness, process, integration, and transformation that best defines open, complex, adaptive systems where emergence and self-organization occur.

Many scientists now ask questions that for years were the province of religion. It is not uncommon to see conferences on science and religion, science and consciousness, science and mind hosted by universities like Harvard, the University of California, and Oxford University. These are academic conferences, not religious ones.

But many would argue that the traditional schism between the spiritual and scientific is not an unbridgeable divide. It is often more a matter of methodology than content. It is not unusual to see contemplative practices both studied and used in university classrooms across the country (see, for example, the programs at www.contemplativemind.org. Studies on love and altruism are now funded by major medical research universities and foundations. Meditation is now an accepted part of medical practice, and there is an increasing number of programs across the country that teach mindfulness and other stress-reducing techniques as part of school curricula.

So while the language of constructive postmodernism and wholeness science may come across as what has been viewed traditionally as anti-intellectual, it is in fact grounded in very elaborate mathematics and philosophical thought. Both authors have found that our students respond enthusiastically to this new research, in part, because the language itself seems to free them to explore various aspects of their lives that have been ignored in much of their educational experience.

As the language of wholeness and connectedness is increasingly absorbed into social usage, it begins to convey a more holistic understanding of the world of experience. Almost every day there is another study that addresses the relevance of our mental state, the positive benefits of meditation, the significance of purposeful living, and the physiological effects of love or altruism or gratitude.

The latest scientific developments show that experience can actually alter DNA structures and that our beliefs and mental models affect how one approaches the practical events of our life. The idea of an ecologically related and interdependent world is almost taken for granted. Each one of us engages in a vast, intangible network of connectivity every day when we use the Internet, and the idea of social networks and group interaction has been forever changed with such inventions as Facebook and Twitter.

Transformation and wholeness are a natural part of life, yet oddly our institutional thinking remains largely ensconced in classical, modernist assumptions. Even as the ancient Greek virtues of mind, body, and spirit become more relevant as they are adapted to new constructs, society still tries to engineer human activity and create technical models that remain largely linear and disconnected from human intention, purpose, and meaning.

Emergent teaching is one way of framing these complex understandings and developments into practical applications. While we would argue for a very different kind of education than what is prevalent in conventional schooling, this book is not an articulation of that vision. Our humble intent is to make some of these ideas more accessible to educators who are constrained by the circumstances that stem in part from substantialist thinking. There are windows of opportunity to integrate emergent teaching within the current instructional contexts. We know this from our own experience and the experience of our graduate students who teach in public K–12 schools.

EMERGENCE AS CONTEXTUAL

Deborah Osberg and Gert Biesta (2008) write of a "space of emergence" which they characterize as participating within a context of radical contingency and response (p. 314). The space of emergence occurs when learners have an opportunity to question, explore, and share their understandings and deepest concerns with others. Emergence means that the whole is constantly changed and transformed by the parts even as the parts, too, are changed. This book contains many stories about this "space of emergence."

To find those spaces where emergence can happen requires a different way of seeing. Our tendency, especially in the West, is to focus and act on that aspect of a problem that seems most apparent, that is glaring us in the face. When learning becomes defined by high test scores, teachers tend to put all the emphasis on fixed results to the exclusion of everything else.

One principal said recently that his district is requiring him to give extra help to those students who are most likely to bring up scores statistically rather than provide extra support to those who most need help. This principal is being forced to do something he feels is not good for the majority of his students.

This kind of fixed focus, without considering the larger whole, according to Ramo (2009), is ultimately ineffective. He gives many examples where effective action resulted from understanding the importance of connective relationships. He suggests that in a dynamic environment, it is the internal factors that often have the most impact (p. 136). Without understanding the context, actions are likely to be misdirected.

Ramo points to a study at the University of Michigan by Nisbett that illustrates how our inclination to fix attention solely on the problem to the exclusion of the context is typical in the West. Nisbett conducted eye-movement studies. He had groups of university students look at a variety of images in a machine that depicted a central object in the center within its environment, like a tiger in the jungle.

The eye movements of the North American students stayed primarily with the central object of the scene. Subsequent questioning of the students confirmed that these students only focused on 25 percent of the picture; they could answer very few substantive questions regarding the context of the primary image (pp. 165–167).

In a similar way, much of education today is fixated on specific outcomes or specifically labeled pathologies while ignoring the importance of the larger context. It is as if the extended relationships that make up the learning environment have little or no real significance.

Lanza (2009), a biologist, makes the point that when developing cell cultures for experiments, he has to focus on creating healthy environments for them to grow. Otherwise they deteriorate quickly and become unusable.

He nurtures the context rather than fixes the cell. It requires a change in thinking not to focus on what we perceive needs to be fixed. It seems almost counterintuitive.

David has found in his drawing class, especially figure drawing, that if the student is encouraged to include the larger context rather than focus on the model exclusively, then the figure itself ceases to be as problematic and becomes unified with its environment and more successfully rendered. Similarly, it is precisely within context that opportunities for emergence occur.

The book includes stories and metaphors as ways to explore how the science behind emergence can be applied to the classroom. These multi-threaded tales create a context to understand emergent teaching in a more personal and meaningful way.

STORIES AS METAPHORS

The concept of emergence is itself a metaphor. Within the sciences of complexity and chaos, emergence is more an aspect of mathematical dynamics than it is an idea. Something unpredictable and self-organizing is put into motion that has no causal factors than can be isolated or predetermined. As an idea that may have large implications, emergence needs to be concretized around human experience. The intent here is to explore these possible meanings through the extended use of story.

The authors feel that stories help us enter those spaces of emergence where the unknown is created and comes to life. The stories we present are not just examples or illustrations but rather working metaphors that allow the reader to examine various aspects, qualities, and occasions where the unplanned, open spaces within the curriculum produced something new and unexpected. These are stories of transformation, not in the sense that we set out to change or alter who someone is but the transformation that occurs when the event creates its own natural outcome.

Stories as metaphors are not explanations; they are indicators. They may or may not tell us specific things about a topic. But the storied events of our lives encapsulate experiences that move our understanding. Kittay (1987) notes that "metaphor is plumbed not for its affective and rhetorical efficacy, but for its cognitive contribution" (p. 2). And Stivers (1990) points out that "the cognitive usefulness of a metaphor comes from its help in reconceptualizing information" (p. 2).

Metaphors provide imagistic markers that move us away from technical abstractions into the world of experience. In this way they provide a process for change. Stivers elaborates on this when he adds that "using a metaphor is the primary way that accommodation and assimilation of information are accomplished—especially accommodation of new experience" (p. 2). Stories as metaphors provide multiple truths that are underneath the surface, always to be seen in the light of our own experience and imagination. They are like multithreaded tales.

If you have ever done "mind-mapping" or "webbing" where you place a concept or idea in the center and create as many associations as you can think of, subsequently creating associations of associations, then you have a sense of a multithreaded tale. Approaching a story by playfully yet purposefully creating multiple possibilities of meanings is a form of textual analysis. Relating those possible meanings to one's life and experience is another form of analysis and also synthesis.

The term "multithreaded tales" often occurs in the literature of applied complexity. Just like conversations, these kinds of stories are nonlinear. In other words, they lead in many directions at once.

The following stories illustrate the use of narrative to explore ideas. They provide a context to show how emergent teaching can occur rather spontaneously and how there is an inherent, nonlinear quality to what happens. The reader may also notice that these stories are "event-centric," where movement and change tend to create the structure that allows something substantive to occur.

Several years ago Sam worked with a small high school for about six months. Many of the students had practically given up on school. This story represents a multithreaded tale of one student.

Joel had been in and out of special education classes over the years. Now in tenth grade he still struggled with basic skills, but more than that, had given up hope. His peers also reinforced the view that he would never be successful in school. As a result, the young man acted out and was identified as a troublemaker. He gained a certain amount of prestige from this, and he projected a tough guy image.

I remembered that at one time he had taken a summer photography class and seemed to enjoy it. One morning Joel came early to school and I had a chance to talk with him informally. I asked about his photography and he became enlivened. He told me of some of the technical things he liked about it and at the end of the conversation I asked to see his work sometime.

Surprisingly, the next day he brought me a portfolio of his photography and with great pride started to explain each piece, going into elaborate detail when he talked about the technical processes he used. He was animated and clearly knowledgeable. I asked if he would mind if I displayed his work in the school. He seemed taken aback at first, and then gave me permission.

Waiting until the weekend, I placed them along a corridor in gallery fashion. On Monday, the kids arrived and immediately noticed the work and who did it. Rather than dismiss it, they spent time looking at each piece. When Joel arrived at school, he was greeted with questions about the photography and surprise that he was so good at it.

The students previously had only perceived him as unaccomplished and not very smart. The tone and level of their questioning suggested that their perception of him was immediately changed. At an all-school meeting, I brought attention to the photography and the quality of the work it represented. Many of the students also commented and you could see a pride in Joel's face that was unmistakable.

This event changed my relationship with this student and began to alter others' perceptions of him. I was able to offer academic help that before had been rejected. His bad behavior became almost nonexistent except for a few lapses.

Through future conversations I learned that he was also an excellent mechanic, so I arranged to bring an old car to school and offered a special auto mechanics presentation for all interested students. Joel served as the assistant to the local mechanic who offered an after-school class. He presented information in a way that all students could understand it, once again showing his knowledge and evident mastery.

Students' opinions of Joel changed; they saw him in a new light. So what began as a simple conversation turned into something transformative and meaningful. No, he didn't immediately increase his reading level or become the model student. But he did apply himself more and made steady progress. Joel was no longer invisible and he became an important member of the school community.

As a multithreaded tale there is no one way to view this story. It can have many different implications and messages. For example, there was an *unplanned* moment that was outside the curriculum. Sam could have overlooked this opportunity if he had focused only on missing homework or Joel's previous history.

The encounter was an *authentic* one where there was genuine interest and a desire to connect. Joel's response in bringing his photographs was also unexpected and led to further conversation and the spontaneous idea to display his work. The story then expanded when his photography was shared with the other students. The larger community played an important role in what emerged when they asked questions about his work. The unpredictable nature of these events *unfolded over time* and had an effect on many students, the teachers, and Sam.

Emergent teaching, then, opens a space where the significance of our knowing, individually and collectively, can develop on its own without rushing to a particular outcome or educational agenda. As teachers a goal is to become more aware of opportunities for emergent processes and creative engagement. A kind of intuitive knowing occurs that is different from the "plan and teach" model we are so used to. Emergent teaching is a process of self-creation and, as such, is transformative at every level.

Our experience with emergent teaching is that these kinds of opportunities are more prevalent than one thinks. It is natural that students would want to interject their stories, questions, and life experiences into the curriculum. Yet often we rush through our work without opening up these spaces where students can be heard, and we miss opportunities because we fail to see how their stories and questions can be expanded and developed into the larger context of learning, which may be deeply personal or open the door to larger creative possibilities. Sometimes this evolves into multithreaded conversations where meanings are discovered in areas we did not anticipate.

The next story shows that a single conversation can open the way to exciting learning. It also shows how the integration of planned and unplanned events can work together. This is Sam's story of Carlos.

Carlos came into my office one day to engage in a simple and brief conversation. I was new to the school and wanted to get to know the students a bit. Carlos was very affable and extroverted and always seemed to have a smile on his face. Even without knowing him, I liked him. After a short introduction of what this was all about, I asked, "Carlos, I really would like to know what your interests are, what you love." A big grin shone on his face as he looked me straight in the eyes and said, "Sam, I love dirt!"

I was grinning back at him now, totally unprepared for that answer. You could see he loved the fact that I didn't know what to say. Carlos went on to tell me that he was an off-road bicycle racer who did elaborate tricks from dirt ramps that sent him high into the air across trenches and ditches. He was part of a semiprofessional circuit and was about to have a major sponsor.

Carlos explained that he had little interest in school and just wished he had more time to play in the dirt. I was quick to point out how the business end of any professional sport required academic skills, but he had heard that pitch before and was not impressed. We talked a bit more and I learned a lot from him about his sport, his dreams, and what he wanted out of life.

I could not get the conversation out of my mind and wondered how to connect his passion for bike racing and jumping to the curriculum in some authentic way. An idea started to form. In collaboration with the math teacher, we met with Carlos to design a dirt ramp where he could demonstrate a bicycle jump to others at the school and the teacher could develop a series of mathematical problems related to her algebra and geometry classes.

Using the time before and after school, we had a team of students build the small course under Carlos's supervision. When the course was complete, Carlos did a presentation describing the sport and the training that was necessary. Then the math teacher made the link to applied mathematics. For a week, Carlos demonstrated his amazing skill and the students created and solved math problems related to the curriculum.

A few days after this event, Carlos walked up to me with his always casual grin and thanked me for that experience. Then his whole demeanor changed to one of great sincerity as he told me that he would never forget it. Walking away, he turned back to me and said, "I love dirt!"

This story illustrates how potent a simple conversation can be when there is an *openness* and a desire to understand and support a student's interests and dreams. In addition, the curriculum was enriched by adapting the content to Carlos's interests. All students benefited by seeing a real-life application of mathematics. They engaged in difficult problems, but the problems had purpose and meaning to them.

Finally, the community itself was enhanced because students could identify with someone's dreams and could begin also to imagine their own. As a multithreaded tale, multiple meanings can be applied to this story and applications to other instructional settings can be inferred. This is the nature of emergence.

This book is itself a multithreaded tale and developed in ways that could not have been predicted. It started as an ongoing conversation between the two authors, and in the process our teaching changed. In a similar way, this book provides a space of emergence where your own stories become part of a larger conversation—a conversation that increasingly needs to take place in education today.

Chapter Two

Indra's Net

The Experience of Nonseparation

Emergent teaching is an alternative way to think about and perceive what teaching can be. If a teacher cannot "see" emergence, she will not notice those opportune "spaces" where something unplanned can be allowed to happen. If there is not some understanding of what emergence is and how to participate with it, then she will be reluctant to stay with uncertainty long enough for it to self-organize into a pattern she can guide or influence.

Davis and Sumara (2006) suggest that what is often called "the teachable moment" is one example of emergence that many educators are familiar with—those times in the classroom when a variety of circumstances brings about an opportunity to shift directions from the planned to the unplanned. It may be a question, an incident, an outside event, or something else the teacher noticed that stimulates a recognition that there are other possibilities than what is planned for and scheduled. Observing a teacher take advantage of these moments is often like watching an artist at work.

The landscape of emergence is often an intuitive response to something that a teacher "feels" is needed but is not evident. Learning how to identify the landmarks of this landscape, though, helps a teacher bring together an intellectual understanding with an intuitive response. This chapter deals with a fundamental mindset that lies at the heart of emergence—the world we are part of is not isolated, fragmented, or static; rather it is connected, relational, and mutually co-constructed.

Einstein stated that the biggest delusion of our time is that we are separate, self-contained, and self-sufficient entities, unrelated to the rest of the universe (in Nadeau, 2001, p. 179) This is our conditioned experience, and because of this, it is difficult to understand how we can be connected in a significant way to things distant and seemingly inaccessible to us, even though nonlocality (connection at a distance) has been both mathematically and experimentally confirmed.

There is an ancient story called Indra's Net that helps us understand the dynamics of nonseparation and the qualities of the universe as an interconnected whole.

> According to the myth there is a net which stretches out infinitely in all directions across the universe. At every node of the net there is a jewel, and since the net itself is infinite in dimension, the jewels are infinite in number. If we now arbitrarily select one of these jewels and look closely at it, all the other jewels in the net are reflected in it. Not only that, but each of the jewels reflected in this one jewel is also reflecting all the other jewels, so that the process of reflection is infinite.

Even though this story is set in ancient India, the visual metaphor it creates is quite consistent with many new scientific understandings. What may appear to be separate and apart is in fact connected to an endless web of relationships.

Goerner (2001) observes that "science as a whole is beginning to discover that you really can't understand much of anything unless you look at how webs create order" (p. 139). She also asserts the "the web view of how the world works creates a radically new framework for thought. Over the next ten to fifty years you can expect a flood of new philosophers outlining the social, spiritual, economic, and political implications of this view" (p. 418).

A web of complex relationships refers not only to the external world but to the mind as well. Zull (2011) provides a holistic model of the brain that he describes as a complex integration of "cognition, emotion, feelings, sensory experience, and motor experience . . . interacting with the environment" (p. 279). He argues that the compartmentalization of much of the current brain research "may be challenged in the future as we develop methods that are designed to discover connectedness rather than separation" (p. 281).

And Siegel (2010) defines mind as an embodied process that emerges as it dynamically engages in interactions among neurobiological and interpersonal processes as well as the natural and technological environment. He developed nine domains of neural integration that together create what he sees as an undivided self. A web of complex interactions that is essentially indivisible and whole is a growing recognition throughout the sciences even as it has been a key understanding in wisdom traditions in many cultures for thousands of years.

What might a webbed view of reality mean for education and how does it apply to emergent teaching? Let's look at three understandings we can take away from the myth of Indra's Net.

1. The universe is inherently connected, relational, and dynamically changing. This idea lies at the heart of emergence and emergent teaching.
2. The story of Indra's Net relates to the self-reflective quality of our lives. If learning leaves out the self-reflective questions and concerns of our students, it will miss the opportunity to be transformative.
3. Just like the jewels in the net, the process of reflection is infinite, continuously creative, and moves in all directions at once. In emergent teaching, multiple possibilities are present, often at the same time.

We will now delve more deeply into each of these points to come to a deeper understanding of emergence and how it can facilitate a more positive and open-ended context for education and learning.

1. The universe is inherently connected, relational, and dynamically changing.

This is exactly how Evans (1998) describes Whitehead's philosophical synthesis of early twentieth-century science.

> He [Whitehead] directs our attention to relationships and the potential multiple effects of events. These relationships, both internal and external, connect, lead to digressions, reconnect in new ways, expand possibilities, and influence each other in myriad linkages. The connections and influences are not linear but web-like. This classic web form displays unity, purpose, relationships, and sequence, but not in a straight line. (p. 63)

Emergence occurs out of the movement and interplay of these relationships. Its outcome is dynamically created in this kind of environment. It is an inherently creative process and has within it an energy that seems to sustain itself in that moment.

Emergent teaching places the teacher within the midst of this dynamism. It is really exciting and enlivening to inhabit this space. Just as the constant interplay among the jewels in the story of Indra's Net is reflective of the creative force of the universe, there is a creative energy present within the relationship among students, the teacher, and their shared environment.

These dynamic forces are always in flux, their relational aspects never fully predictable, and this is the foundation for emergent teaching. When complexity is given an open space, creativity will happen. Something unexpected. A new direction. A deeper sense of the same place.

There is a fun activity that Sam has used with many different kinds of groups of different ages, backgrounds, cultures, and languages to have them experience how emergence happens naturally out of this kind of interconnected dynamism:

Groups of three stand together in close proximity. One member of the group is selected to be the "starter." That person begins to slowly create an original story.

For example: "Once-upon-a-time-there-was-a-BIG-tiger,-and-one-day-the-tiger-went-down-to-the-river-to-drink.-and-guess-what-he-saw. . . ." As the story-teller in each group speaks very slowly, the others in the group mimic the same words at the same time.

When the teacher says "Change" the person to the starter's left continues creating the story in the same manner as the other members of the group mimic her. The change of storytellers continues intermittently until the teacher says "Change and finish." That person brings the story to a close. The activity is usually filled with laughter, playfulness, and a rather ridiculous story.

But several conceptual ideas are illustrated. The story was told by everyone and no one. In other words, the particular story that was created would not have been the same without the input of each individual in the group. The timing of the directive "change" actually contributed to the outcome. The initial conditions and the person who started the story made a big difference as did the one who finished the story.

Another lesson that participants notice is that there are certain skills that become really important for the activity to work. One skill is deep and intense listening. Because each group member is mimicking the words at the same time, being present and fully engaged is a necessity.

A willingness to give up control is something that many struggle with. Some want the story to go in a particular direction but they have to relinquish their version of the outcome when the next member takes the lead. Each member can influence the outcome but not control it.

Those who experience this activity also observe that they are able to be creative and spontaneous when the need presents itself. So the activity becomes an experiential metaphor for emergence, beginning with the ideas of connectivity, relationship, and dynamic change.

In emergent teaching the context for learning becomes as important as the content. The context of learning includes the way the studio or classroom is set up. Is it inclusive? Does it contain elements that speak about the lives of teachers and students outside the classroom? Does it reflect the multiplicity of relationships that make up their lives, their ecology, their family, their country, history, or biology, all of which create a rich environment for learning? These questions provide a foundation for a different way of thinking about what we do.

The impact of the peripheral environment on learning has been well documented (Caine et al., 2009). From music, to art, to aesthetics, we know that the human physiology is affected by the interaction of internal and external conditions. Humans experience the world within a context, yet oddly, the consideration of context is rarely given a significant place in preservice training. And the contexts that matter most often lie at the periphery of our attention.

Ramo (2009), in writing on the practical applications of complexity thinking, emphasizes the significance of seeing the larger context. He states that "little in the current discussion of our shared problems suggests the radical rethinking our world requires. There is now hope . . . but the basic architecture of ideas and theories necessary to back up such difficult work remains profoundly underdeveloped" (p. 10). A webbed view of reality that allows for the interplay of context and unbroken wholeness is an important and necessary place to begin.

Perceiving this kind of interconnectedness and relationship, however, is not always easy, especially when we are taught to focus primarily on the fragment, the isolated fact, the formula unrelated to context. Sam recounts a teaching story where teachers began to really see and understand interconnections and wholeness:

> It was early fall and the sun was already bright as a class of graduate students gathered to begin a discussion on holistic education. When I mentioned that we were going outside for a while they looked quizzical, then excited. I asked them to spend a few minutes alone in "aimless wandering," which is quiet, unstructured meandering in a natural environment. Next they were invited to let their attention be drawn to a natural object and observe it more closely.
>
> Using their observation and imagination, I asked them to notice the boundaries that seem to exist between them, the object, and the environment. I then asked them to notice and follow what happens when these boundaries are released from their perception and the process that occurs when we follow the dissolution of boundaries. Finally I asked them to become aware of their own presence as an observer and to consider what happens perceptually and psychologically when the event of being there is added to their observations.
>
> When the students gathered together again they shared their experience of this process: Some went imaginatively inside the object to observe its interior workings, others into the far reaches of the universe. Some used their scientific background to rethink processes like photosynthesis and a plant's connection to the sun or our own inhalation of oxygen from trees and the tree's absorption of oxygen that we exhale. The soils, minerals, and water needed by plants extended the complexity of their interconnections.
>
> As each of these connections was extended further, everyone realized that we create separation in our perceptions that are not naturally there; and with it there was a realization of a wholeness that could not be contained, or conceptualized.

Emergent teaching, based on the principles of interconnectedness and poetically described in the myth of Indra's Net, allows for the interplay of the individual and the community. It provides for the natural development of the creative mind through process, and it recognizes the power of interactions not only in the classroom but also in the larger community. As with Indra's

Net, the important point is that anything and everything is inherently connected, and because it is inherently connected every circumstance and interaction becomes part of the learning environment.

This interconnectedness also has an ethical component, because one realizes that one's actions affect the health of the larger community. This can create a foundation for social awareness.

In practice, thinking relationally opens up an extraordinary range of possibilities for the teacher. She is able to apply a wide spectrum of materials and experiences to her teaching and is more accommodating to ideas from others in the community. History, for example, comes alive when we include genealogy and our ancestral roots.

Writing on the importance of metacognition, Zull (2011) concludes that

> A learner's awareness and insight about development of his or her own mind is the ultimate and most powerful objective of education; not just thinking, but thinking about our own thinking. It is when we begin to comprehend our own thought that we can sense progress in our journey toward mind. This comprehension may be our highest and most complex mental capability. (p. 259)

From a perspective of nonseparation, the role of the learner is an integral part of the contextual dynamic and cannot be ignored or done away with. Thus, the self-reflective nature of learning is the second focus of exploration.

2. Life is self-reflective.

As in the metaphor of Indra's Net where every node is reflected in every other node, each of us is reflective of everything. Understanding that we are constantly reflecting, that we are part of the world around us, has become an established view of quantum mechanics, even if it is an uncomfortable one for many scientists to acknowledge. Dyson states that it appears that mind, as manifested by the capacity to make choices, is to some extent inherent in every electron" (in Laszlo, 1996, p. 148).

The inherent interrelationship of the whole within every part and the part within every whole that is posited by quantum theories is illustrated beautifully by taking an ordinary slide projector and removing the lens. When a slide is placed in the carousel all one can see is white light shining on the screen. But if you place a magnifying glass anywhere in front of the projector, the entire picture is projected in each discrete area of light that is highlighted. In other words, it shows that every particle of light contains the entire picture.

The holographic quality described here is also demonstrated by a single DNA molecule, where one's entire DNA information is contained in every individual molecule. In addition, quantum scientists have long agreed that, at least in quantum experiments, the observer cannot be separate from that which is observed. "All things in the world—quanta and galaxies, molecules, cells, and organisms—have 'materiality' as well as 'interiority.' Matter and mind are not separate, distinct realities; they are aspects of a deeper reality that has both an external matter-aspect, and an internal mind-aspect" (Lazslo, 2004, p. 149).

So from this perspective nothing can be studied that does not in some way refer back to the one studying it. Therefore, learning about anything is an inherent opportunity to learn about oneself. This becomes fundamental in emergent teaching.

The concept of emergence implies that transformation takes place naturally and continuously. It is through self-reflective inquiry that we come to realize this. Applying this inquiry to a deeper understanding of who one is, each of us shapes the world even as we are shaped by it. This ongoing and never-ending process constantly changes and redefines who we are and the world we live in.

The self-reflective nature of emergent teaching is illustrated in a story of one of David's high school students, Joshua.

> As part of a sculpture class, students were given an assignment to build a *retablo*, which is a movable altar, and at the same time examine their assumptions about religious iconography. Each student was asked to reflect on the process and write about their experience. Joshua did not have much training in the technical aspects of sculpture, especially in terms of how materials often are used to translate or explore ideas. But he had a definite interest in the subject and was willing to challenge himself. He summarizes his experience:
>
> "My sculpture started with an idea spawned from the assignment given to the class, to create our own version of a retablo, an altar in a box. My idea was that God is in a box—at least it is a box when most people encounter spirituality, particularly if it must be manifested in an altar to be understood. The commonplace action of institutionalizing religion can often place boundaries upon people's minds and consequently their spirituality.
>
> "I attempted to manifest this in a sculpture by creating a figure that is bound and contained within a box that is obviously too small for it. Thus, the box is constricting to the spirit that is supposed to live within it. However, the project had to evolve further than that. After all, religion, spirituality, and faith are not bad things on their own terms. Even the institutionalization allows for large numbers of people to relate to a side of themselves that might otherwise be ignored.
>
> "This gave rise to the next idea about my project, that one is controlled by the things one is content to live with. I began to look for things to signify satisfaction that could be used ornately within the box. I chose to use money because I thought it would speak well to most people by communicating the idea that satisfaction with commodity can place boundaries upon one's life.
>
> "In retrospect, as a result of critique and introspection, I am able to see where my project is weak. Commodity in the form of money is too easy. The beauty that I saw in the idea is much more complex than money. I wanted to

incorporate thought as commodity, and satisfaction with enough thoughts and enough ideas can control one's desire to learn or to think. The same can be applied to ideas of peace, liberty, justice, education, beauty, and more.

"Still, I struggle to find any image that can be utilized to represent this aspect of life. At times I think I need to stop trying so hard to find it. It is beyond being manifested in a physical world, yet must exist within it. Thus I wonder whether to keep searching through long lines of complex thought or to sit back, and if I don't look too hard, I will see how to incorporate it into an art form."

Joshua started by using the containment of the retablo as a metaphor for the containment of God in most religious practice and how that containment limits our view of the world. But he also goes on to say that religion has a positive function in that it can create wholeness both individually and through community.

So he is already stepping outside the confinements of the assignment and at the same time literally stepping outside the "box." As educators, we have to be open to the possibility that our thinking (as reflected in assignments and projects) is too narrow and that we might have to modify our views in order to engage the student's inquiry.

The retablo is an established sculptural form in traditional art and yet, for Joshua, it became a powerful metaphor for him to explore himself. The space of emergence was provided by the provocative nature of the assignment, the open dialogue during critiques, and the opportunity to move beyond the concrete product by writing a reflective paper on the process. Process is not the same as emergence, but it often can provide the space for it to occur. As in the story of Indra's Net, Joshua tapped into questions and perplexities of his own journey.

Emergent teaching invites students to relate their learning to their questions, interests, experience, and their deepest concerns. In this way, the curriculum naturally emerges from within the process of this inner-activity as well as the interactivity of the group.

More generally, this means that in the classroom we need to give time for contemplation, where we reflect on issues relating to life. This can mean quiet time, meditation, Socratic inquiry, listening—whatever is appropriate to the environment and provides a safe place for self-reflection. We have found that students who participate in these practices are more invested in the process of learning since it comes from their individual and shared insights.

3. The process of reflection is infinite, is continuously creative, and goes in all directions.

Human activity in the world is sometimes portrayed as a pebble being thrown into a pond. The ripples from the pebble go in all directions at the same time just as many of the results of our thoughts and actions may actually be unseen and unknown. The following experience by Sam illustrates some of these principles:

> I was watching it rain recently from a lakeside cottage. Sprinkling at first, each drop of rain created its own circular life-world as it pierced the surface of the water, followed by a small upward splash and tiny circular ripples which soon dissolved into other ripples created by many thousands of drops of rain.
>
> As I looked across the lake it was as if the whole surface was trembling, and with the rain coming down harder the sky, water, and lake became indistinguishable. When the rain stopped, the heat of the day returned and I could see a soft vapor rise across the lake filling the atmosphere with humidity, and the beginning of a new cycle of transformation and change.

The summer shower and its effect on the lake is an apt metaphor for what happens in emergent teaching: it is not a singular or linear process but has lingering spheres of influence that become hard to distinguish or classify. As teachers and educators, we often have very linear concerns.

Teachers try to help students learn particular skills or information and help them understand concepts that will shape their thinking and understanding. They are trained to assist learners through a variety of techniques, to organize what comes first and second, and to assess whether or not the student has learned what was taught to a sufficient degree. These kinds of linear concerns become habitual; it is sometimes difficult to even conceive of teaching apart from them.

Buhner (2004) has observed, however, that "we in the West have been immersed in a particular mode of cognition that is defined by its linearity, its tendency to reductionism, and its insistence on the [mechanization] of Nature" (p. 1). This way of thinking about experience has affected all of us and all our institutions. Sociologists would say that part of us becomes bound up in the institutional structures we participate in.

The structural elements of institutions embed mechanistic and linear ideas into day-to-day practices that dominate everyone's lives, the expectations placed upon us, and the processes and content accepted as legitimate and authoritative. It has become a closed system of truth that is self-perpetuating. It is a system of thought that now depends on ignoring or leaving out anything that does not fit within its parameters.

The consequences of continuing this way of thinking and perceiving the world can be disastrous. Educational institutions perpetuate many of these ways of thinking through the curriculum and content, the organization of the school schedule, and many of the accepted teaching and evaluation processes.

Teachers constantly face this conflict and often miss opportunities for emergent teaching with its "lingering spheres of influence," struggling to find ways to truly discern how the process of learning integrates with who students really are. We had the opportunity to see an alternative to this kind of learning in an art project which David planned a few years ago in which he introduced students to sand painting:

> The project developed in ways that we could never have predicted and beautifully illustrates the principles and practice of emergent teaching, which as you will see "goes in all directions at once."
>
> David had prepared large, square forms and students were asked to divide them into four (one quadrant for each student) in which they would create a sand painting that characterized some key aspects of their locality—the place where they lived. These characterizations could be from their experience, their feelings, or more obvious demarcations of history, geography, or culture.
>
> In the center where the quadrants met was a circular area in which students would bring actual earth or physical artifacts that symbolized "place." David talked about the history and process of sand painting and demonstrated ways students could use color, images, and symbols to create their pieces. While the students were free to express themselves creatively and independently, we asked that they do their work in a way that created to a sense of unity.
>
> One group of students lived in a mountain town that had recently been devastated by forest fires. Many people they knew had lost their homes and the entire community was deeply impacted by these fires. They decided to bring ashes that represented various areas that were burned and placed these ashes in the center of the sand painting.
>
> At the end of the project, they shared their work with the rest of the group and described with great emotion what it symbolized for them. The students then poured the sand into large five-gallon buckets and took them outside to an undeveloped part of the campus close to the mountains where the fires had burned. We asked them to give the sand back to the earth, in remembrance of the communities that were devastated by fire. David and I were surprised how moving this ceremonial aspect of sand painting was to them, and when we processed the experience, most of the comments had little to do with the art processes. Rather, all the students made connections to various parts of their lives, their histories, and the places where they lived. The process of dismantling their beautifully realized sand paintings was extremely hard, but they saw in it the temporality of life, and as they returned the sand to the earth there was a sense of completion.
>
> Two teachers, Stacy and Evelyn, who lived in the mountain community ravaged by fires were profoundly impacted by the sand painting experience. In discussing the fire with their own students there was a shared sense of pain,

loss, and the fear of reoccurrence; so they had their students make simple drawings of their experiences and share them openly. They noticed a kind of healing in the process that was more profound than in earlier discussions about the fires.

Because of the students' response, Stacy and Evelyn decided to offer an after-school workshop where they brought charcoal ash from the burned trees and had the students use it to draw scenes from their experience. The event was so powerful, students and parents asked for more workshops.

Not feeling knowledgeable in various art processes, the teachers requested help from some artist friends in the community. Now with additional help, students mixed clay with ash and created pottery. They continued to use charcoal as a medium. Stacy and Evelyn also introduced painting, created poems, short stories, and plays. The larger community became involved and experiences were created for adults as well, and out of this the healing of an entire community took place.

The lives of their students were so affected that Stacy and Evelyn had to radically change their class plan to allow the students to have the emotional space they needed. Eventually, these intense experiences changed not only the way these teachers conceived of teaching, it changed their lives. They were now asked to share their experience with other districts. Their students came with them to demonstrate their incredible art-making but also to share their stories. And ultimately these two teachers based their masters' theses on different aspects of this process and the transformative changes that took place.

This story, just like Indra's Net and the raindrops falling into the lake, illustrates that emergence is not linear. What emerges goes in all directions at once, influencing everything and being influenced in return. From the planning of a simple sand painting activity and the introduction of the skills needed to do it, emerged the healing of a community and left an indelible mark on the teachers who allowed themselves to be agents of transformation.

David created a space where teaching was not limited to the application of skills. Rather, students were invited to bring their own life-worlds into the process and to create a community where their stories could be honored and shared. In this process, the curriculum disappeared and something magical and unanticipated emerged.

Stacy and Evelyn's project shows how this kind of creative possibility can affect an entire community. It became "unbounded" when they allowed the process to unfold naturally. As members of the community became involved, the project took on new and different dimensions, each shaped by the circumstances that created it. It became a natural part of the classroom conversation in ways that did not have to be forced or planned. Its creative potential and impact could not really be measured, but as a result of the project significant healing occurred in the community.

Emergent teaching, by creating spaces for transformation, paradoxically, helps us see connections everywhere. This nonseparate view of the cosmos offers a foundation for emergent teaching and a different way of perceiving the world. It is a perception that is full of potential, information, and meaning, providing new ways to understand and organize the curriculum.

Thus, we return to three lessons we can learn from the story of Indra's Net:

1. The universe is inherently connected, relational, and dynamically changing. This idea lies at the foundation of emergence and emergent teaching.
2. The story of Indra's Net relates to the self-reflective quality of our lives. If learning neglects the self-reflective questions and concerns of our students, it will miss the opportunity to be transformative.
3. Just like the jewels in the net, the process of reflection is infinite, continuously creative, and goes in all directions at once. In emergent teaching, multiple possibilities are present, often at the same time.

The way we perceive the world is critical to the ways we act within it. Therefore, the perception of a nonseparate cosmos affects who we are and what we do. Cultivating this perception in our lives and our classrooms is both the challenge and the power of emergent teaching. Subsequent chapters in this book will show how these simple but complex principles can be applied to teaching and how we can create the open space and processes that are needed.

Chapter Three

Process from an Emergent Perspective

Event-Centric Teaching

The idea of process is not new to educators; for years there have been shifts of emphasis between the prominence of content or process in instruction. Few would deny, however, that both are important or, perhaps more aptly, that the two are embedded in each other (Crowell, 1989). But what does process mean from the perspective of emergence? How does this view of process reflect the principles of nonseparation? How might it change the way we think about instruction?

There is a wonderful poetic line that was used by Francisco Varela to describe the basis for what he and Humberto Maturana called enactive theory of cognition: "Wanderer the road is your footsteps, nothing else; you lay down a path in walking" (Antonio Machado in Thompson, 2007, p. 13). In the beautiful imagery expressed here we are shown a situation in which the road or path did not exist before the walking. It is like crossing an open meadow after a fresh snow. The path becomes your own footsteps. Looking backward, you see where you have been; looking forward, the path is an open question, full of creative possibility.

Key to understanding process from an emergence perspective is that it is nonlinear in terms of both how and what becomes the product. We educators are notorious for breaking something down in terms of process steps and then having students follow those steps. This practice can indeed be helpful but it is not emergent. In addition, teachers will often introduce particular process skills that a student can use to investigate a topic or develop a product of some kind. Again, this can be extremely helpful in the overall development of disciplinary understandings, but it is not necessarily what process means from a perspective of emergence.

Thompson (2007) notes that "strictly speaking, it does not make sense to say that a property emerges, but only that it comes to be realized, instantiated, or exemplified in a process or entity that emerges in time" (p. 418). Let's explore what this might mean by considering an assignment David gave his high school sculpture class.

> At the beginning of the year I asked my students to go out into nature (the Idyllwild Arts Academy has about 250 acres of relatively undisturbed forest land) and find a location that they felt a strong connection with. They were to build some kind of structure there out of the materials that were at hand. This was the first stage of the project.
>
> Then they were asked to visit the site every month for the rest of the school year and document any changes. This documentation could include photographs, journaling, drawings, or other means. One of the stipulations was that they were not to manipulate the piece or the surroundings in any way, even if the sculpture was destroyed. The documentation should be purely observational.
>
> Over the time period of the assignment these places became sanctuaries for the students and their observations became more acute as they began to pick up on the smallest of changes in the environment, including animal tracks and broken twigs. As the year progressed, the sharp distinctions between art, nature, and the happenings of life were less apparent as the students became absorbed in the very process they were observing.
>
> At the end of the year, the students were asked to present the documentation as part of their final project. While each student's experience was unique, the separation that was present when they first began the assignment eroded over time and was replaced by an intimate connection with the sculpture, the school, and the natural environment. The students acknowledged that their lives had become part of the process of documentation and they had become a part of what they observed.

Looking inside the elements of this story several things stand out in terms of emergent teaching. One important aspect is there was no specific outcome expected other than a consolidation of the experience of documenting the changes in the sculpture over time.

Part of the meaning of process here is that something was put into motion; an ongoing event was created. The fact that the events *over time* were allowed to develop on their own is significant. The act of going each month to sit, observe, and document actually defined the outcome. The product existed entirely within the potential of the process. As Oliver (1989) explains, process includes the imagining, the selection, and the ordering as one interrelated dynamic.

A second characteristic of emergence present in the story is that the assignment deliberately had minimal boundaries in terms of rules. This allowed and encouraged the students to make choices, decide what was important, follow their interests, and draw their own conclusions. Each visit presented them with something new to notice, investigate, and reconsider. In complex systems, boundaries (and the rules they impose) tend to shift because they are constantly exchanging information with the environment and they constitute a part of multiple networks at the same time (Davis and Sumara, 2006). The rule structure here was consistent with the openness of the activity.

Third, the assignment had interactive layers that necessarily included each other. For instance, the students began by creating the sculpture. They were immediately engaged with the surrounding environment and needed to imagine, conceptualize, and use the materials they found there in a new and creative way. As they visited the site throughout the year, they added new layers to the experience.

Also, they watched something created be altered with the passage of time. Individually each student came with a new set of experiences each month. Life imposed itself onto the project, especially as students chose to visit more often to seek refuge or sanctuary from the demands and troubles of being a teenager.

The modes of documentation changed and offered the students a different set of lenses to view their experience. They also had to take into account the unintended consequences of the project's effects on them as a person, student, and artist. An additional layer was to choose how to organize the loosely collected documentation as a whole and to decide what was important to present to others. The whole and the parts intermingled and both had to be considered.

Then there was the presentation itself and the subsequent interaction with other classmates as they reflected deeply on their own and each other's experience. These interactive and conjoined layers created a context of complexity for other possibilities to emerge. Emergent processes need this kind of variability.

A fourth element of emergence illustrated by this story is the concept of recursion or iteration. These terms refer to a pattern of self-similarity where in math, for example, the output of one equation is the input for the subsequent equation (Doll, 1993). Recursive processes are a basis for fractal geometries and other nonlinear mathematics.

In this story, recursion occurred each time the students revisited the sculptural space. Not only did they observe something new but the whole of their previous experiences was actually a subtle part of the new one. The idea of revisiting can be used very effectively in the classroom to enhance learning and is a necessary ingredient for emergent teaching.

PROCESS AS TRANSFORMATION

The story also provides a window into transformation and change. Process, from an emergence perspective, is not a view of specific behavioral change that is planned and manipulated by the teacher but rather a view of change as ongoing, ever-present, and constantly reorganizing itself. This notion of process, when applied to education, leads inevitably to a transformative view of learning. Nothing really stays the same. Even conclusions are tentative in that they merely represent an illusion of stop-action—where one's thinking is at a given point in time.

The students not only observed change, they were part of it. And making meaning out of the whole process was yet another aspect of transition and reorganization. When all the documentation was presented there was still one more consolidation of experience that was represented by the entire community. The transformative outcomes were unique to each student's construction of meaning, not to a viewpoint of a particular authority. Students created a relationship with their experience that was qualitatively different from a set curricular expectation.

What becomes evident is that emergent teaching requires a new orientation to the concept of process. In emergence, process is not an action that is merely instrumental; process is itself an integral aspect of the structure as it comes into being. It reflects the principles of nonseparation in that there is no object apart from process; there is no subject apart from its ongoing construction.

This represents an entirely new way of viewing the world in our time. The world has shifted from being a noun to being a verb. Dewey knew this; Piaget knew this; Bruner knew this (Doll, 1993). Artists have always known this intuitively. And as we shall continue to show, it has been a growing recognition in our scientific understanding of the world for the past seventy-five years.

PROCESS AS EVENT

In ancient Greece and in ancient China a sense of process in an event-filled world was not an uncommon view. For example, Ames and Hall (2003) explain that in ancient China "particular 'things' are in fact processual events, and are thus intrinsically related to the other 'things' that provide them context. These processual events are porous, flowing into each other in the ongoing transformations we call experience" (p. xxx). And Heraclitus, the ancient Greek philosopher who lived around 500 B.C., wrote:

I see nothing but Becoming. Be not deceived! It is the fault of your limited outlook . . . if you believe that you see firm land anywhere in the ocean of Becoming and Passing. You need names for things, just as if they had a rigid permanence, but the very river in which you bathe a second time is no longer the same one which you entered before. (www.spaceandmotioncom/philosophy, retrieved November 17, 2009)

This view of the world as events is consistent with Oliver's (1989) explanation of process as he interpreted Whitehead: "For process there is no perfection only continual change: the becoming, transforming, and perishing of occasions" (p. xx). Oliver felt that the more a student was distanced from meaningful experience, the more fractured and irrelevant learning would become. He argued for a grounded or ontological knowing where students felt connected to what they learned and to the community around them. This was the experience of the students in David's class.

THE MANDALA

Emergent teaching challenges us to *follow* what happens rather than *control* what will take place. In the story below, the authors were co-teaching a graduate class taught at a wilderness reserve. Try to notice the aspects discussed above that characterize process from the perspective of emergence. In addition, the story illustrates the complex nature of process, transforming events, and the importance of following what happens.

You will notice that there are multiple processes that take place in an almost layered fashion, but those decisions for the most part emerged rather than being preplanned. You will notice also there are subtle differences between "process" and "processing" as they subsume one another.

We asked our students to construct a mandala-like form from objects found in the wilderness. David introduced the aesthetics of the mandala and gave examples of its cultural history. Since we wanted to provide an experience that would help us explore the fluid nature of process and its emergent qualities, we pointed out that there is a difference between theorizing about an object and participating in its creation.

So, in an open space outdoors, the students were asked to create a large, perfect circle and divide it evenly into segments for each person. An inner circle was also created with an opening to the East, a common feature of Navajo sand paintings. Each student was asked to walk alone in nature and find objects that they connected with which would be used to create individual segments that combined meaning, creativity, and aesthetics. Afterwards we would introduce each segment and celebrate the whole. Then the mandala would be disassembled and each object returned to its original location.

The students were really excited to begin. We asked if they needed our assistance with anything but they requested that we only observe and be available. Almost immediately there were problems in how to approach the task. It seemed that everyone had a different opinion of how to proceed.

Some of the more natural leaders in the group stepped up to try to reach a consensus but there were arguments even among them. There was a visible frustration building as no solution could be agreed upon. Some students withdrew emotionally; others were clearly agitated. We watched and waited but no one asked us to step in.

At the height of chaos there was a sudden regrouping and a recognition that a different kind of interaction was needed. Rather than trying to convince each other of their ideas, they started listening to various suggestions. There was an almost instant agreement on a course of action and the structural portion of the mandala took shape quickly.

What occurred later, however, was perhaps even more interesting. In the evening, as we sat around a fire pit revisiting the experience, we examined the dynamics of the art experience and explored the meanings that students had created for themselves. It was clear that what students experienced was quite diverse. They made all kinds of intellectual connections and found many things to relate to their teaching and learning.

Then they went deeper. There were hurt feelings and conflicting emotions. There were memories of past events that tapped into withdrawal and anger. There was honest sharing and genuine listening, tears with stories of personal pain. But in the end a tremendous bond of loving support had been established.

David and I felt a heavy uneasiness, however, because we sensed that the emotional bonding was somewhat tenuous; even though students expressed their feelings honestly and without bitterness, we knew intuitively that there was much more under the surface. We were also questioning our own judgment, wondering if we should have stepped in during the most chaotic moments.

The next day we decided to share our uncertainties with the students and invite them to probe the experience more deeply and include the interaction around the campfire. We asked them to explore the relationship of their own choices, judgments, and reactions to the overall event. Rather than see themselves as separate from what happened, we asked them to examine their actions in relation to the whole and see if something constructive could be learned that would benefit themselves as well as the group. The discussion went much deeper this time.

The insights and understandings that emerged from the students were remarkable. The depth of their perceptions and their willingness to learn from what happened is something neither of us will forget. Following the students in this instance opened up an incredible opportunity to learn at the deepest levels.

Later, we decided to look again at the intellectual implications of the mandala activity to see if exploring the emotional context made it easier to make conceptual connections. It seemed that a freedom to go deeply had been established that allowed our students to reveal their intellect and creativity.

They suddenly were expressing significant understandings of open and closed systems, feedback and process, some of the essential ideas of chaos and complexity theory, and the insights related to holistic teaching and experiential learning. They expressed how learning deeply just did not happen in most school settings, and they recognized the vital importance of experience and process.

Many of the elements of process discussed earlier can be seen in this story as well. The activity was *event-centric over time*. There were minimal rules imposed on the activity but the ones that were established (creating a perfect circle, dividing sections of the circle evenly according to the number of participants, etc.) served to provide a focused expectation while also posing a problem that needed resolution and creative energy.

Just as in the earlier story, there were multiple interactive layers that added complexity in both scope and depth. Recursion occurred at the camp-fire discussion and the group processing later the next day. The experience was also revisited (iterated) many times throughout the class and in subse-quent courses as well. Each time there was some new connection to the event, some newly consolidated insight, or new relationship to an idea.

And finally, a transforming change occurred that no one could have pre-dicted. The community seemed to take on a different identity and individual-ly the students became very aware of each person in the group.

In emergent teaching the teacher becomes comfortable thinking about process in these ways and looks for opportunities to involve students in experiences that create natural complexity where the student becomes part of the learning. The teacher must follow rather than lead for this to happen. In the next section, ways to facilitate process of this kind will be discussed.

FACILITATING PROCESS

The stories above are meant to illustrate various elements of process from a perspective of emergence. As multithreaded tales, they represent metaphors to be plumbed for meaning and to stimulate the reader's own imagination. They are not presented as models of instruction or as a demonstration of how to teach. We are well aware of the constraints that most teachers endure. We know that most schools are in urban or populated environments and may not have access to wilderness settings or specialized concentrations of study. So this section will address more specific instructional tools that can be applied to a variety of settings, grade levels and subject matter.

In general, we have found four factors to be important in making process a part of instruction: participation, engagement, choice, and time. The idea here is not to offer a process model but rather to illustrate how these practices can help create the complex conditions that emergence requires.

PARTICIPATION

Participation opens up opportunities for students to interact with one another; participation here is more nonlinear, a sense of conversation. When students interact with a sense of purpose and the teacher uses the interaction as part of instruction, an environment for emergence has been established.

In traditional settings it could be briefly reviewing in small, informal groups the previous day's activities or content. Or it might involve pairing students for a one- or two-minute discussion on a relevant question. Sam has helped high school teachers in various subject areas create discourse groups to enhance critical literacy skills like analyzing, synthesizing, articulating, and writing.

Such activities are nongraded, time-efficient, experiential, and open. These practices are simple, brief, and uncomplicated and when followed by a larger, general discussion in which student's ideas and perspectives are incorporated, they provide opportunities for teachers to *follow* the students that enhance the conditions for emergent possibilities to occur. In more open settings students can begin to shape the curriculum by their own questions and interests, openly discussing and balancing what is most important to them individually and collectively.

Often there are opportunities to create short physical activities that illustrate some important concept like creating a geometric shape using arms and hands or photographing geometric lines and features around the school. Or in writing, students in groups might be allowed to share an extraneous event from the day that is woven together into an integrated story that they then perform which illustrates the basic architecture of beginning, middle, and end. Afterwards, the short plays are critiqued in terms of the elements of style, then revised, and redone.

Essentially, the writing process has been demonstrated through an alternative medium. Given the exigencies of time in a normal school day, these activities may not happen often, but they become meaningful and memorable experiences to draw from and elaborate upon. In addition, students can be allowed to narrate content as a story, thus reinforcing their own understandings but also expressively relating this to others.

These activities initiate process. Instruction becomes more authentic because it combines student experience with content. Thus the content will be shaped by the students' response to it.

ENGAGEMENT

Engagement is a more complex form of participation, often incorporating a problem-based or project-based assignment that provides students the opportunity to apply or creatively reconstrue what they are learning. These kinds of assignments can be made as out-of-class projects with periodic time given in class for students to collaborate or receive teacher guidance and assistance.

Sam uses book clubs in some of his courses. Students choose among several different books and do individual reading. They then meet to discuss the readings with others who have chosen the same book. Each book club group prepares a creative way to present their book as well as the substance of their thinking to the rest of the class.

David recently shared a story that describes a project-based assignment that has multiple layers to it and embeds a number of important skills related to the discipline of art, specifically sculpture. Notice how by layering various aspects of the assignment, students became more deeply engaged and how the complexity of the process was enhanced.

> In a beginning sculpture class, students are largely unfamiliar with the use of materials and the development of representational form. They have little experience in breaking down form into increments and analyzing the shape, texture, and minute details that constitute an object. I asked my class to replicate a personal, ordinary object in terms of is texture, form, and exact size. They worked on this independently during class, and I was able to assist them with particular aspects of the process.
>
> As the students completed their object they shared them with others, recollecting the process, reviewing their decisions and choices, noting the difficulties, and getting feedback from the class. This allowed them to learn from each others' work. They were clearly excited by the assignment.
>
> I asked them next to place their sculptures in an ordinary public place and film people's interactions with the piece. One student had replicated an old purse and placed it in the cafeteria line. The reactions to it were curious, unanticipated, and sometimes hilarious. The students became fully engaged in the filming, trying different locations, filming the filming, and capturing multiple aesthetics. The students edited the film as they shared the documentation of their installation. Then they created composites and integrated the documentation with the sculpture in now a different presentation.
>
> Next, I provided yet another layer to the project, sending students to a local thrift store looking for contrasting objects to their original sculptural form which they had to integrate into a new piece. In adding this layer, the students transitioned from representational form and installation to conceptual art. Because of the contrasting elements, textures, size, and forms, the new sculptures provided a very different kind of challenge.
>
> The ideas that informed the new work were as important as the form itself. The students' work was remarkable and showed a maturity of both thought and skill development as each of these layered processes unfolded.

When students are engaged in a complexly layered process over time, the conditions for emergence to occur are ripened. The teacher now helps the students not only recognize the disciplinary elements that are critical but also perceive the emergent qualities of the process, their own thinking and decision-making, the multiple relationships that are apparent, and the ways that what may have seemed fragmented were in fact parts of an ongoing event that was whole unto itself.

As demonstrated in the story, layering is one way of creating complex conditions. Sam often demonstrates this by introducing students to a complex African drum rhythm. First, there is a solid rhythmic beat that holds the time. An additional layer of rhythm is then added; then another, and another. As each layered part contributes to the other, complexity is created.

When students begin playing off these established rhythms something quite remarkable and original is produced. At the point where layering becomes original and self-organizing, emergence occurs. Emergent teaching is about creating these conditions.

CHOICE

Choice is a third key element of facilitating process. How does choice relate to the concept of emergence and emergent teaching? It is important to remember that emergence occurs in an open, adaptive, self-organizing system. This means that information from the environment is constantly being processed and used to adapt to ever-changing conditions. A technical term for choice when speaking of complex adaptive systems is *agency*. There is a "choosing" among multiple possibilities. Process occurs in an environment of choice. It is in the act of choosing that adaptation and transformation happen. This is especially true of human beings. As Ramo (2009) says, "we are not passive; we can move" (p. 108).

Sometimes we teachers think the more structured an activity is, the more successful it will be. That is because we hold on to the idea of a tightly controlled curricular agenda. Our society perceives teaching as giving to students what they are expected to learn and then holding them accountable to learn it. This view of teaching is reinforced in our institutional structures and in the organizational decisions we make. Hence teachers are trained to control and manage both the curriculum and the students.

In almost all natural learning situations in the real world or even at the highest levels of academia, some kind of choosing is involved in learning. Sam's students provide an example of this:

> A few years ago several of Sam's graduate students were asked to explore areas of choice that would be appropriate for their classrooms. Four or five of these students were teachers in a correctional facility for incarcerated youth.

Most of the students they taught were members of gangs and had extremely violent backgrounds. The facility was the antithesis of choice, and so the assignment seemed almost ridiculous to these teachers. Nevertheless, they met together to assess where choice could be offered and they created an experiment to see if even small choices had any impact on their students.

The choices were absolutely minimal, such as choosing the color of a magic marker or making miniscule alterations in the schedule. Then additional choices were added that included a one-minute timed conversation with a peer. Because some of these kids belonged to competing gangs, little opportunity to talk with each other was usually given for fear of fights and verbal outbursts. But at the end of several weeks, the graduate students reported that nothing they had done previously had had such a positive impact on the classroom community as these opportunities for choice. These small acts of choice-making provided a sense of respect and dignity that had not been a part of the students' constrained environment.

Choice, however, is often interpreted educationally as freedom, or conversely it is used to give the appearance of freedom by manipulating the options— "You may choose to do A or B," where both A and B are closed or predetermined options. Even the immediate example above concerning the incarcerated youth has some of this notion of choice. But choice from a perspective of emergence is related to a contrasting theory of knowledge.

Doll (1993) sees choice as tied to the exigencies of one's experience. It is interactive and dialogic and emphasizes creating knowledge rather than discovering it; negotiating meaning rather than verifying it (p. 126). So, choice in the sense of an assignment is boundaried by the wholeness of the particular project. Now of course, choice can also be used politically and be an important part of the culture of the learning community. Choice provides the openness necessary for change, adaptation, and self-reflection to occur. It is a creative event and is part of the final outcome. In terms of emergent teaching and an understanding of what facilitates process, when a teacher provides authentic choices she opens up the environment for something creative and original to happen.

TIME

The idea of process used here is *movement through time*. Picture yourself having a conversation with a good friend at a café. If you don't have very much time, the formalities of the exchange are pretty quick. Your conversation may focus on a recent event or it may be more of a random chatter until one of you has to go. But if you have the luxury of time, the conversation lingers around certain topics, drifts away and then comes back. The focus may be a prevalent theme or interest between the two of you, or it may be a dominant preoccupation of one or the other.

When there is no hurry, you may notice your surroundings a bit more—who else is there, what is happening—or get something to eat. Topics start to change and become more random. You may start to notice things in a different way or become more natural in your responses. Perhaps the periods of silence are longer. As the time increases, you may start to think about what you have to do next and thoughts of worry or pressure or anticipation start to creep in, even as you are talking about something else. The point is, time affects the dynamics of process. It allows for change to occur more naturally or, if the time period is short, more deliberately. When one is engaged in an activity over time there is more adaptation to changing conditions and circumstances; there is more interaction, and a shifting of purpose and priorities is often present.

The longer one thinks about something, the more it becomes self-reflective, complex, ambiguous, then crystallized. This is especially true when there is feedback, discussion, and dialogue with others. For Doll (1993) this kind of "'recursive reflection' lies at the heart of a transformative curriculum; it is the process which Dewey, Piaget, and Whitehead all advocate" (p. 178). It is focused conversation over time that allows transitions, shifts, and transformations to take place.

To facilitate process, a teacher must provide an appropriate level of time that includes some kind of purposeful revisiting of the questions, decisions, observations, and insights that bring the person into focus. It is not time in and of itself that is necessary in emergence but rather it is the *movement* of time that produces the existential qualities of meaning and significance to surface.

In one of Sam's philosophy classes he has his students reflect upon and contemplate various questions that emanated from the early Greek schools of philosophy (see Pierre Hadot, Ancient Greek Philosophy, 2005) for ten minutes each day throughout the term. His students are all teachers, many are single parents, and a number of them are taking several graduate classes concurrently. The most difficult requirement about the assignment is finding five or ten minutes a day to do nothing but contemplate various questions related to their deepest concerns and aspirations. Repeatedly they complain about the busyness of their lives and the demands placed upon them by almost everyone. At the end of the course, when they share the experience of doing these contemplative exercises, almost without exception they thank him for "forcing" them to carve out those five or ten minutes of solitude. This time becomes a respite for many of them in which they can nurture their inner lives and find direction for themselves in a complex and busy world. The following is representative of some of the responses.

Recently, after doing the contemplative exercises, a teacher commented to me that she recognized the need to spend more time gazing inward. She commented that "these exercises brought up questions in my mind about what is important in my life."

Another teacher observed that "the philosophical exercises helped me gain perspective on what I thought was a chaotic, out-of-control world. In reality, the chaos was what I created in my own mind. Now I can honestly say much of my stress is the stress I create."

This kind of exercise provides the opportunity to notice things about oneself and see more clearly the workings of our minds. Turning attention to our inner lives invites the subjective to be a part of intellectual processing. Questions eventually become possibilities. This transition, however, takes time.

As Rilke reminded us, "Be patient toward all that is unsolved in your heart and try to love the questions like locked rooms and like books that are written in a very foreign tongue. Do not now seek the answers, which cannot be given you because you would not be able to live them. And the point is, to live everything" (Rilke, 1903). So while emergence is derived from complexity, the human aspect needs time to process, simplify, and self-organize. This is true of any substantive change.

We live in a culture of speed. We spend much of our time just trying to keep up or move ahead. The stress in our daily lives is often related to the fast pace of life or filling time with more and more activity. This affects the quality of living; it also affects the quality of learning. Guy Claxton (1997) in *Hare Brain, Tortoise Mind* argues that our society has emphasized what he calls d-mode thinking—the kind of thinking that demands a quick response that is rational and urgent, precise, purposeful, and conscious. He calls for us to rehabilitate the slower modes of knowing.

These slower modes require incubation, playing with images, metaphors, and meanings. They engage us in being receptive to our unconscious processing as well as the conscious. This kind of thinking leads more often to wisdom and insight; it relates more directly to our deepest concerns. We often refer to this slower mode of knowing as ruminating, contemplating, or pondering. Emergent teaching accentuates these ways of processing one's experience.

The most recent research on brain functioning supports the importance of taking the time to go into more depth in terms of substance and application. The perception-action cycle of learning (Caine et al., 2009) draws on research on the cerebral cortex and the executive functioning of the brain. This is the locus of higher cognitive activity where creative possibilities, problem-solving, and social and emotional connections are organized. Unless students can use what they are learning to make decisions and applications, they do not learn.

Also, highly successful educational alternatives like the Khan Academy emphasize learning at the student's own pace. This requires the development of a less hurried mode of learning and teaching. Learning that allows the individual to be a part of the process encourages the student to linger over a project, to see it from various perspectives, compare alternative solutions or applications, to understand relationships to other issues, and to enjoy the process of creative learning.

So, process is *movement over time*. In terms of emergent teaching, it requires a teacher to view the world as constantly moving events in which each of us inevitably is a participant. The more one accepts this participation and engages in it, the more the opportunity to influence and learn from experience increases. Choices and decisions create a direct relationship to the subjective qualities of our humanity. Subsequently, the opportunity to reflect, revisit, and dialogue about our experience over time adds to the depth and substance of learning.

In the next chapter we will discuss the related notion of nonlinearity and how important it is to an understanding of emergence and emergent teaching.

The Shape of a Snake

Nonlinearity and Emergence

This may seem like an unusual title for a chapter on emergent teaching, but it provides a visual image of a *meandering* line. The sinuous, wavy motion of a snake, often circling back into itself, has been used throughout human history to depict discovery, uncertainty, curiosity, and reflecting backward while moving forward. This labyrinthine pattern is nonlinear and is evident throughout nature. Even Einstein used the example of a meandering stream to discuss the complex mathematics of the helical.

Our society has conditioned us, though, to appreciate the straight line. Going from point A to point B without detours represents efficiency, practicality, value. Clear, unambiguous language, goals that are realistic and achievable, objectives that are sequential, concrete, measurable, and irreducible—these are the attributes infused in our psyche, embedded in our organizations, and are part of the hidden curriculum in our schools.

This linear structure can also be seen in suburban developments with row after row of houses, all built with a common floor plan. It is evident in our supermarkets and department stores as aisle after aisle of products line up before us, often with nothing in particular catching our attention. Linearity is valued in our automated industries, in strategic planning, in approaches to time management and systems of evaluation and accountability.

Linearity, however, is rooted in technical thinking; it is rarely evident in nature. Natural systems are irregular and unpredictable and exhibit self-similarity and recursive behavior (Meadows, 2008; Holman, 2011). Living organisms are not linear or deterministic. Nor do our brains think in linear ur neural networks don't operate that way (Zull, 2011). So one gue that the prevailing educational worldview is in many ways in- ent with the natural capacities of human beings to learn.

asmussen (2010) states that "learning as a conscious activity and teach- g as a communicative social activity both belong to the category of complex, emergent systems" (in Osberg and Biesta, p. 15). By treating learning as mostly technical and linear, educators are in fact imposing mechanical solutions on open, adaptive, growing, developing, creative, meaning-seeking individuals. No wonder so many students are disaffected from the educational system!

Emergence is nonlinear and recursive, but what does this mean for a teacher who is trying to address the needs of students and be responsive to the demands of the curriculum? How can the concept of nonlinearity be understood in a way that helps rather than confuses? The shape of a snake may provide an image, but what is its relevance for teaching? This chapter will address these and other questions.

WHAT IS NONLINEARITY?

Nonlinear dynamics and mathematics are used to investigate interrelationships, connections, and blends of similarities and differences (Smitherman, 2005, p. 154). Nature "happens" through nonsequential processes where information "feeds back" into the system and self-organizes (emerges) into something new. This makes emergent outcomes unpredictable and time-based. They are divergent and generative (Smitherman, 2005). Prigogine and Stengers (1984) tell us that "non-linear reactions . . . are virtually the rule as far as living systems are concerned" (p. 153). This means that nature is engaged in a constant process of creating itself anew in the ongoing flow of time.

Nonlinear processes are different from randomized events in that they reflect how interconnecting relationships feed information back into the system, thus affecting not only the system but also everything around it. This is often referred to as *positive* feedback. In other words, new information is taken in by the system which allows it to choose or adapt to changing conditions (Davis and Sumara, 2006).

A familiar example of this would be doing a Google search. Once a topic is identified you have immediate choices to investigate. And if one is encouraged to follow subsequent interests wherever they lead, then there will be a meandering quality to the investigation.

No two searches are likely to be the same even though they may contain similar information. If you were to plot the information from four or five people searching the same topic, there will be both a divergence and expansion of information and also a likely set of similar patterns; so the process would be nonlinear. However, to make sense out of the search, another process of consolidation and organizing must take place. Here, the questions, the interests, and the dialogue around the topic feed back into the search, even as new questions and searches are generated.

Nonlinear processes are all around us, yet for some reason we educators tend to force the idea of learning into a preconceived linear structure. This actually takes learning away from the learner, unless one's view of learning is memorizing particular content.

Closed, in contrast to open, systems depend on *negative* feedback loops. This is discrepant information indicating the discrepancy of the system from the goals set for it. Most mechanical systems are "closed" and operate with negative feedback. Familiar examples would be a thermostat or the cruise control on your car or even formative testing in a classroom. Because the goals are predetermined and there is little room for alteration, linear process-es are mostly used. While both positive and negative feedback loops are useful depending on the context, emergent teaching focuses more on positive feedback systems that are inherently nonlinear.

Sometimes there is a mistaken assumption that nonlinear processes re-main in a state of chaos and disequilibrium. What is interesting, however, is that living systems are always moving toward some kind of coherence and consolidation. So while the outcomes may be open and unpredictable, a new state of closure will be produced. Emergence is all about transformation and change. It is the way nature evolves.

Holman (2011) explains that emergence occurs through some kind of *disruption* of the familiar which triggers a state of differentiation of the elements or processes of a system. At this point an alternative, more complex coherence begins to arise. This is reminiscent of Piaget's notions of equilib-rium, disequilibrium, and re-equilibration (Doll, 1993).

Humans are designed to make sense of their experience, consolidate the patterns they encounter, and create meaning based on the biological, soci-ocultural, and psychological conditions that inform them. *Active processing* is a term used in the Caines' brain-based learning model to stress the educa-tional importance of giving students time and processes to consolidate what they have learned (Caine and Caine, 2001; Caine, Caine, and Crowell, 1999)—in other words, to bring order and meaning to the multifaceted and multimodal world of experience.

Nonlinearity is natural to learning as it moves the system (the learner) to a new state of coherence resulting in novelty and change. This process con-nects new knowledge to what was previously known, but it's not just that something new has been added; the *whole* is no longer the same as it was. This new whole encounters the world from a newly situated place. Because the new whole is different, everything is different. Nonlinearity is a critical understanding for any discourse on transformation and transformative learning.

The authors have used the term *meandering* to represent the nonlinear process of discovery, consolidation, and willingness to follow the unknown. Emergent teaching depends on these qualities. It is the willingness to follow the ambiguity of the open-ended question, the insights that come from reflective observation, and to cultivate an awareness of how we are experiencing the present that allows a teacher to work effectively with the nonlinear. The story below shows how some of these characteristics became evident in one of Sam's classes.

Recently, I was teaching a two-week class on the neurobiology of stress for educators. On the first day, I invited the students to spend twenty minutes outside by themselves just taking in the day with no agenda in mind. They could stroll the beautiful campus, lie down in the grass, or follow their natural interest wherever it led them. I called the exercise *aimless wandering*.

The students had a surprised look on their faces; this was not a typical academic activity and since it was the first day of class, they were a bit taken aback. I had to clarify that there was no expectation behind the activity, except to simply enjoy the day. We had been examining how the sources of stress in our lives are a result of our perceptions, not the circumstances. We had discussed patterns in the environment that created outside expectations in which we often felt powerless to change. I had presented some of the neurophysiological effects of prolonged stress and how these affected performance and learning. So with their minds full from these previous discussions, I sent them outside to let the day come to them.

When the students returned, they were refreshed, energized, and hungry for similar types of experiences. They were surprised how quickly they became fully engaged in doing absolutely nothing. Yet these students also came back to class full of ideas, reflections, and insights from their experience. It seemed almost counterintuitive that so much came from "nothing."

Our discussion revealed how uncomfortable we have become in our society with nonspecific goals and the openness of genuine exploration and discovery. Our curriculum is completely packed with going from A to B as directly and quickly as possible. Time to meander, explore, question, and reflect just isn't part of conventional education. And yet these capacities are critical for intellectual development, innovation, and problem-solving.

I continued to build aimless wandering into the schedule throughout the two-week course. Each day was different, but certain patterns prevailed. First, students were drawn to deep reflection during these times. Some chose to journal or write poetry, others sat quietly, while yet others needed the physical activity of walking. But a constant theme was looking into the center of their lives.

Second, they saw things. Some observed things in the environment that they had never paid attention to before. Some students noticed patterns in their lives that were unproductive or unsatisfying. Others developed a clearer sense of direction or a vision of specific projects they wanted to work toward.

And third, these students consolidated ideas around the course content, crystallized their personal understandings, and had insights about how the material related to their personal and professional lives. Interestingly, the personal and professional was not a neat division and could not so easily be compartmentalized as we often try to do. Some wrote to me after the course sharing how they have incorporated some form of aimless wandering into their daily routines.

As Sam's story illustrates, students typically begin to personalize their learning when they are invited to do so. They seem to have a natural inclination to blend the subjective and objective together. This is an important pattern for educators to pay attention to, for it is an indicator that the personal and subjective are necessary aspects of learning that is meaningful and significant.

Meandering provides students the freedom to pay attention to what they find interesting and to allow a destination or outcome to emerge organically. A teacher can build this quality into almost any assignment, especially as extensions that encourage and give students permission to apply, explore, or create. Meandering creates opportunities for questioning and processing. It requires openness to the nonlinear process of discovery. And it requires the willingness to follow where questions and interests lead.

This places the teacher in a facilitative role where guiding and suggesting replace directing and insisting; where the use of feedback and questioning helps the students go deeper to where the subject matter and the personal intersect. Importantly, what often begins with open, nonlinear features will almost always self-organize toward increasing coherence and structure where linear goals and outcomes establish themselves naturally.

This is especially significant for new teachers to understand because there is frequently a fear that the differentiation will get out of hand. Creating a broad thematic that loosely organizes the content or the projected assignment allows the necessary freedom that emergence requires while also providing a conceptual focus for the teacher.

One middle school social studies teacher the authors work with creates a parallel curriculum project each year that incorporates a trip to the Museum of Tolerance in Los Angeles. She creates a lengthy time frame before and after the visit for students to explore their interests, develop questions, discuss issues inside and outside of class, and even involve their families in their thoughts and ideas.

This allows the teacher to follow what emerges in the discussions, notice the kinds of questions that arise, and create a discourse around the related issues of bigotry and intolerance that are part of students' lives today and the society in which we live. Each year the general focus is similar but the students go in new and unique directions. All this takes place while adhering to the day-to-day requirements of moving quickly through the textbook on U.S. history.

In some contexts a nonlinear approach can be a natural part of conventional curriculum. The development of units, for example, lends itself nicely to a meandering kind of format while still addressing core standards and skills. The authors like to think of curriculum as a loosely focused conversation over time. This perspective will be developed more in a later chapter, but here the significance is related to the relationship between openness and unpredictability (conversation) and imposed expectations (standards).

A former graduate student of ours who taught a third/fourth grade combination class used questions to guide her own initial thinking and later posed open-ended questions to her class. Since the broad topic of "community" was included in the grade level curriculum, she wanted to use it as a vehicle for her students to engage in substantive exploration over time. She was inspired by a principle in the International Earth Charter that reads "Recognize that peace is the wholeness created by right relationships with oneself, other persons, other cultures, other life, Earth, and the larger whole of which all are a part" (Principle 16F). This holistic perspective would provide the boundaries for the unit and the purposeful foundation from which to begin. The teacher began asking of herself: Are there alternative ways to communicate (art, drama, music, technology)?

- Can instruction occur outside the classroom?
- Can resources from the community be incorporated into the discussion?
- How can I promote students' appreciation of diversity?
- Are there experiences I can structure that will help deepen students' understanding? Are there ways to layer these for depth and substance?
- How can the class's sense of community be deepened through their participation in this unit?
- How can I help students process and consolidate their individual and collective experiences?
- What are the core standards that relate to this topic and how can they be embedded in activities and assessments?

These questions are not unusual in and of themselves. They are conventional to most unit planning. But notice how the teacher (any teacher) would immediately be immersed in a nonlinear process of her own. Typically, as initial ideas are generated they will be free flowing, loosely boundaried, and inconclusive.

As more information is gathered and as personal interest grows in one area or another, certain options will open up while others will close. Gradually, a teacher will consolidate the disparate options and structure them into a rational and sequential plan with objectives and outcomes, time frames . . . Stop!

First, observe how emergent the planning process is for the teacher, how natural and commonplace nonlinear thinking is. It is much more a part of our actual experience than most of us realize. Next, although emergent processes are evident in this example, notice how the planning is moving quickly toward a linear model with the heightened probability of predetermined outcomes and methodologies. So before allowing the linear model to take over, teachers can look deeper still at these nonlinear processes.

Another way to think about what is happening is through the lens of *openness, inquiry, and consolidation. Openness* provides the loose boundaries and the uncomfortable uncertainty that is needed. *Inquiry*, the way we are using it, organizes the possibilities around relevant questions, the need for new information, and personal interests. Finally, *consolidation* narrows, understands, and seeks to apply these to what is perceived as needed or what seems most important.

Notice in the example how many times this process of openness, inquiry, and consolidation is likely to have been repeated, each time enfolding the previous conclusions into the next set of considerations. Thus, using the technical terms *recursion* and *iteration*, it is possible to get a sense of what "enfoldment" really means.

Now let's provide a new layer of complexity. Suppose the teacher above collaborates in a joint unit planning process with a grade level team or with colleagues in a professional learning community. While the degree of complexity is immediately apparent, the emergent process of openness, inquiry, and consolidation will occur once again.

The system has now been redefined and the connective elements are increased, and the broader range of inputs and possibilities are also expanded. Nonlinearity will once again be evident in the initial conversation, and ideas will likely go in all directions at once. New questions and interests will be proposed, rejected, and accepted, and new attempts to consolidate and create closure with linear conditions will be made.

Depending on the size of the group, the conversation may be unwieldy at first, so one can already begin to see that the process itself becomes a critical part of whatever outcome emerges.

It is important once again to stop yourselves before being engulfed by the linear model. The natural urgency to consolidate and provide closure must remain tentative and ambiguous for emergence to act as a transformative process. Emergent teaching is a continuous process of opening and closing. Open uncertainty is an underlying quality that persists throughout emergent teaching.

Needleman (1986) provides support for this view, arguing that the willingness to "live within the question" is essential for the development of meaning. Each time the process is opened up it adds another layer of complexity. And it is this layered complexity that creates the creative chaos necessary for emergence.

In our illustration of a teacher in a third/fourth grade combination classroom, the nonlinear planning has so far been limited to the teacher. What happens when it begins to involve the students? In this case, the teacher provided some basic information for her students to read and discuss, and then from that discussion students generated questions.

- What important role do we play in our community to make changes for a safer, cleaner, and healthier Earth?
- What can we do as a classroom to understand the importance of taking care of our Earth?
- What types of activities can we plan for our school to be involved in and more aware of taking care of the Earth?
- How can we work together as a family to take better care of the Earth?

The teacher organized new information and resources for and with the students. She arranged for a field trip to a recycling center, invited several guests to make presentations, and incorporated music and arts activities. The Earth Charter emphasizes "one human family—one earth community" so she introduced the students to the idea of going green. This resonated with them.

Students became involved in individual and group projects. Using the information generated from their inquiries, they decided to create a weekly newsletter informing parents how to be friendlier to the Earth. From this emerged voluntary participation and interest from the parents who organized a beautification project with the children to create a Zen garden outside the classroom.

All of this caught the attention of others at the school, and the class initiated an "issues day" where the entire school would address issues of interest in the Earth Charter. The class extended their interests by creating a website to help others become "green." Parents subsequently established a leadership group to plant flowers and trees throughout the community. The school extended their involvement by creating a school-wide Recycle Week. All this from a group of third and fourth grade children who were allowed and encouraged to become an integral part of what was being studied!

Had the teacher limited her unit to the prescribed one or two weeks where she controlled all the information and outcomes, none of this would likely have occurred. It was by remaining in the midst of the process and continually opening it up to new information and possibilities that an entire community was affected.

Emergent teaching *opens, inquires,* and *consolidates* only to recursively repeat that process by enfolding what was previously learned and extending it once again to new contexts and new information. Also notice the active engagement and agency by the students who were motivated by their intrinsic interests and questions. Their subjective responses became a significant part of what was learned.

In addition, there were both prescribed and emergent outcomes and a natural and meaningful integration of disciplines. The assessments were authentic and criterial according to the context. The teacher trusted that the meandering nature of the nonlinear process would lead to outcomes far greater than she could have designed alone. Each layer of complexity created for and by itself new capacities and potentials for learning.

Meandering creates opportunities for exploring, questioning, and processing. But it requires *openness* to the nonlinear process of discovery. It also requires the willingness to follow the *inquiry* of students' questions and interests. And even as processes are created that help students make sense of and *consolidate* what they learn there is recursive invitation to take what was learned to a deeper level of substance, application, and meaning.

This places the teacher in a guiding and facilitative role. However, the meandering shape of the snake also symbolizes the inescapable influence of the subjective on how and what one learns. Examining this quality of emergence offers another perspective of emergent teaching.

EMBRACING THE SUBJECTIVE

Sam's account of a vacation experience illustrates the self-referential and self-reflective nature of human experience. Self-reference is part of all open, adaptive, complex systems. Seeing subjectivity from the perspective of emergence leads to some nuanced understandings that can be useful in emergent teaching.

> Mine were the first footprints on the beach that morning. Each step I took sunk at least three inches into the wet sand. The surf was loud with enormous curls showing glints of aquamarine just as the sun was apparent in the sky.

I sat facing the ocean, eyes closed. The warmth of the sun mingling with the cool breeze left an exquisite sensation on my skin. The coming and going of the waves seemed to match the cadence of my breathing. I was full and empty at the same time. Thoughts were at first contained, then uncontained. Feelings moved from emotions to sensations. I was experiencing the experience.

This afternoon I walked along a trail on bluffs several hundred feet above the surf. Craggy rocks were visible along the entire coast and the white sea foam accented the shoreline for miles. The waves were cresting at what seemed to be 12 to 15 feet, and as I looked out to sea I noticed they formed uniform walls of water one after another like columns of a marching band. Amidst this orderly and predictable formation was the chaotic "happening" of the wave itself. As I gazed at the vastness and listened to the incessant drone of the waves I felt a connection that did not need words.

From a cognitive perspective of emergence, subjectivity implies perceiving the world through the lens of one's experience and perceiving oneself in terms of one's perceptions. There is an obvious circularity here that is intentional. "The organization of an organism comprises numerous circular causal loops, such that every component is definable only in terms of the total organization to which it belongs, whereas the total organization is definable only by specifying those components" (Thompson, 2007, p. 144). Like the story of Indra's Net in chapter 2 this may provide a useful image to understand the natural holism involved in subjective experience.

Biologically, when one learns something new, dendrites and brain connections are enlarged and increased respectively, thus altering the learner's physiology. Yet, one's neurological mapping becomes "plasticized" over time, meaning that the mental circuitry conditioned by the physical and sociocultural nature of experience remains largely unchanged (Zull, 2011; Caine and Caine, 2011; Cozolino, 2010).

Through processes of self-reference where previous information and perceptions are altered or challenged, the learner's cognitive mapping is reorganized. This is not automatic, however. It often requires the unlearning of perceptual categories before new learning can find relevant reference points. These reference points comprise the individual's subjective experiences.

Learning is not just about taking in new information *about* the world; it necessarily includes the learner's subjectivity or *consciousness*. "Consciousness and cognition are both understood to be distributed across the entire organism embedded in its environment" (Davis et al. in Osberg and Biesta, 2010, p. 109).

Emergent teaching, therefore, provides opportunities for students to apply and integrate what they learn to their own life-worlds. The term *life-world* here reflects the embodied nature of all learning and the inherent connection between the individual and the world of experience. "Consciousness does not emerge from the independent and isolated workings of individual brains but, rather, is an elaborate process that arises as the conscious self and the 'other' interweave and enfold one another in a complex—that is, co-determining and self-transcending—choreography" (Davis et al. in Osberg and Biesta, 2010, p. 110). It might be added that it is a "choreography" that is nonlinear and often recursive.

One's "subjective" experience, therefore, is part of one's "objective" experience and vice versa, because from the perspective of emergence these simply cannot be separated. They constitute an interacting whole. The authors have used the understandings of self-reference to create experiences where students can not only consolidate what they are learning but learn about themselves at the same time.

An easy way to think about doing this is simply by directing one's focus of attention. For example, focus your attention on the sensation of your clothes touching your skin. The sensation is very obvious once attention is placed there but most of the time we are unaware of it. Next, focus attention on the tension in your face and allow that tension to relax. Now, focus attention on a real occasion in which you felt genuine love or gratitude. Feel those feelings and gently hold them in your consciousness. Still further, focus your attention on questions or thoughts that are occurring as you read this book, allowing yourself to be immersed in whatever arises. Each new intentional focus produces a range of different experiences. Learning cannot be separated from one's awareness. And awareness always integrates one's subjective and objective worlds.

Schwartz and Begley (2002) emphasize the significance of focused attention, stating that it "can redraw the contours of the mind, and in so doing can rewire the circuits of the brain, for it is attention that makes neuroplasticity possible" (p. 339).

Educators can easily encourage as well as direct students' attention to be focused on their own metacognitive processing. When introspection and awareness are incorporated into a larger discourse, the teacher finds herself once again in the midst of nonlinear *openness* where deeper *inquiry* and *consolidation* of recurring patterns or new insights can lead to transformative change.

THE LABYRINTH

The image of the shape of the snake certainly applies to the structural form of a labyrinth and the meandering experience of walking; its path brings to mind the nonlinear and unpredictable nature of life. We have used labyrinths in courses we have taught together and also individually with our own classes. It is always amazing to discover the range of experiences students have; some are intensely personal and others are connected to a larger sense of a shared humanity.

We use labyrinths as a way to experience the nonlinear, to highlight the subjective quality of experience, and to create a strong sense of community. Invariably the result is much broader. David's account illustrates these qualities and their impact on students:

> I work primarily with the seven-circuit Cretan labyrinth, which is relatively easy to build but big enough to get lost in. I spend some time discussing the history of this ancient knot and how it appears in many different cultures. What I emphasize mostly is the experiential side, which includes the planning and building process, and the challenges of collaboration. This is a focus in all my arts classes.
>
> Once the labyrinth is built and we are ready to walk it, I give very little guidance on how that should be done. I feel that the students need less rather than more information about this so their own experience can be as fresh and original as possible. A commentary by a high school student from Korea reflects this:
>
> "Walking through the seven circuit labyrinth is just like taking a quick glance at life. Seeing a process in which a baby grows up and becomes an adult, slowly gets old and dies, and then another baby in a different part of the world will be born and then the process starts again.
>
> "Before I started, I felt excited and was looking forward to the journey. Just like a child full of hope when everything around them seems new and exciting. The middle part of the walk is like the process of learning and experiencing different tastes in life. There is a path for you to follow that seems so straightforward yet so curvy at the same time. There are times when we experience happiness and sweetness in life and also times when there is bitterness and frustration.
>
> "When I reached the center of the labyrinth, the first feeling that came up was the feeling of completion. It is like I had reached the end of a process, the ending of a life. And everything that I own and that I experience came together at one point. But after this feeling I realize that this is not exactly the end of the journey. I had just gone through only half of it; there was still the other half for me to travel. This made me think of the cycle of life. We are born, we live, we die and then we are born again. This cycle goes on and on forever and never stops."

This is a poignant example of the self-referential nature of our experience and how we create personal narratives that give meaning to it. The high school student above showed a wonderful openness in her walking of the labyrinth. Notice that she uses the words "experience" and "process" frequently. The connections seem so spontaneous and unpremeditated. It was moving to notice how everything came together for her when she reached the center of the labyrinth and this became her ground zero—a place that clarified the rest of the journey.

The nonlinear aspect of teaching was also recognized deeply when Sam had graduate students build and walk a labyrinth. What originally seemed frivolous for one student turned out to be surprisingly profound:

> For me, the course came together while walking the labyrinth. I thought that walking it would be easy. I watched as others methodically made their way through the maze of natural pieces in just a few minutes. However, when it became my turn I realized very quickly that I was experiencing stress. My stomach tightened and I became a little dizzy. I had to focus my attention on my stomach to relax it [an example of focused awareness].
>
> Then the fact that other people were watching me took me to a state of self-consciousness, my perspective of being judged. As I began to walk I found myself wanting to look ahead to see if I was moving in the right direction. However, each time I looked too far ahead instead of focusing on where I was, I began to lose my balance.
>
> Oftentimes, in my personal life I forget to enjoy the journey and focus too much on the destination. This also relates to my school life because it is easy to get caught up in teaching the entire curriculum and rushing the learning experience for students. I realized that I felt the most confident and comfortable in the outer rings of the labyrinth. It was as the path became narrower that I became more uncomfortable. I don't think it's stretching it too far to say that this correlates to the fact that we need to spend time outside and spread out. The confines of a classroom or a school building can be very stressful in and of itself.
>
> As I approached the innermost ring of the labyrinth I quickly became distraught because it appeared as though I was moving away from it instead of closer to it. Many times the lessons of life and the classroom don't happen the way I would have planned them, but after the experience has happened and I can reflect back on it, I know that I wouldn't change anything.
>
> This was my first time both creating and walking in a labyrinth. It was the perfect culmination to a class that has taught me to notice my own needs, make changes to improve my well-being, and in turn create a more positive environment for my students.

The nonlinear, meandering shape of the snake that recursively circles back into itself is once again observed in this teacher's experience. Her self-referential insights are extraordinary and reconfirm how we apply experience to the meaning and purposes of life.

A final example of the labyrinth is when one of the authors' graduate students took her experience of walking the labyrinth into her own classroom. As a high school English teacher, she was assigned a linguistically and ethnically diverse class who were not connecting with the classical literature they were expected to study and learn. The class happened to be struggling with Homer's *Odyssey* at the time that this teacher first experienced the labyrinth. She realized that the meandering journey of the labyrinth in many ways mirrored the journey of Odysseus.

She had her class create a labyrinth on a blacktop surface outside the classroom. After walking the labyrinth they began to relate their experience to that of Odysseus. Not only did these students, many who were recent immigrants, make immediate connections to the literature, they branched out to discuss their own life experiences.

The dreams and aspirations that they held and hoped for seemed far away at times, just like walking the labyrinth. But they discovered that the journey leads toward the center of oneself and in that center resides the resources to move back into the world and, in the words of T. S. Eliot, "to arrive where we started / And know the place for the first time." Yet this place is no longer the same because the person inhabiting it has found their own renewal. This teacher entered that space of emergence where openness, inquiry, and consolidation were allowed to flourish and where a layered complexity was created that not only informed the subject matter but had a transformative effect on students' lives.

OPENNESS, INQUIRY, CONSOLIDATION

This chapter began with an acknowledgment of how a linear mindset pervades our institutions and society. Built upon the values of efficiency, this mindset fragments one's perception of the world and one's subsequent experience by focusing on delineated outcomes, fast-paced linear sequences, and accumulation of objectified information. It may be useful to assess and measure, but this mindset leaves out much, perhaps most, of what it means to learn.

Emergent teaching opens us to new understandings of what learning means and how transformative it can be. When students are given the space to be *open* in front of their questions, bring together experiences and information that guide their *inquiry,* and *consolidate* what is important and meaningful then they are equipped with a process that can be replicated throughout their lives.

These qualities are apparent as one of David's high school students begins to describe a large drawing that depicts a running, disassembling man and in the process enfolds the larger significance of what he has learned about both art and life:

> When you see the man in pieces, is the man falling apart? Or is the man coming together?
>
> I believe it is both. He comes together as he is falling apart.
>
> My drawings and sculptures represent how I feel about the flow of life.

Once we truly begin to learn, we take away in order to build, cutting out the nonessential that hinders us from seeing the truth underneath.

I have noticed that when I started to make my first drawings, there were many things that hindered me from being clear. There was the fear that came from my constant judging of how the picture looks. It is like focusing on one-fifth of a certain activity. When my mind was focused on that particular one-fifth, my attention to the other four fifths was not there. Another element was thoughts unrelated to what I was doing. As my skill increased over the years, I realized that it was the result of my putting aside unnecessary elements: sculpting away what I didn't need so my spirit could be released.

During the process of drawing, there was a stage where I focused too much on adding to the original form. I felt as if I was too concerned with that particular aspect of my drawing. I was in part working against what I felt as I added and added. Next thing I knew I was literally sculpting away the form and at the same time getting rid of what I didn't need mentally.

The form is falling apart to form itself. Just as our old bodily cells die and new cells come forth.

These drawings represent this journey and how I got to where I am today.

Chapter Five

Fostering a Learning State of Mind

Play, Joy, and Irreverence

All things counter, original, spare, strange.
—Gerald Manley Hopkins

The exploration of emergence up to now has focused on many of the principles that come from complexity and chaos theories. This chapter will begin to address some of the conditions that support emergence in the classroom. Being playful and open are essential attributes for creative learning.

One of the conditions for emergence occurs when teachers and educators can relax and put aside many of the unnecessary obligations that prevent us from truly experiencing and sharing our creativity. Once the urge to be creative is activated one may be compelled to question conventional educational mandates, especially if they are overwhelmingly restrictive and limit the quality of our interactions with students.

Cultivating a perspective of play, joy, and irreverence can take practice; we teachers are habituated to fill our lives with seemingly urgent concerns and activities and forget why we entered the field of education in the first place. Of course it is important to strive for excellence but if it comes at the expense of integrity, humor, and creative insight, we are not really at our best—in truth we are diminished.

Integrity means honesty in our interactions, but it also has another meaning closer to integration: "to combine with, to make whole." This is the potential that lies within emergent teaching, which integrates teacher, students, society, and environment in a single process of becoming. From integration comes creative insight that once experienced and validated through action has its own momentum.

The landscape of emergence is in essence unchartered territory. Like a surreal landscape it often contains unusual features that are not commonly associated with pedagogy but that in the context of emergent teaching are indispensable. Learning requires a playful, open state of mind. Emergent teaching embeds these qualities in questions, activities, and assignments.

In this section we will give examples of how play, joy, and even irreverence can become part of an emergent landscape that is full of color and insight. Unlike previous chapters where the emphasis was on the theoretical underpinnings of emergence, this chapter will focus on stories that illustrate the look and feel of emergent teaching.

A PILE OF DIRT, AND THE FALL OF ROME

The first story depicts a kindergarten class that came to Idyllwild Arts Academy to do art:

> On this particular day we ordered a pile of dirt to be delivered so the children could build a city on it. They were given various raw materials like wood, cardboard and clay to build with, and it wasn't long before they were feverishly building houses, towers, castles, kennels, bridges, tunnels, ponds, streams, fences, garden paths, and all manner of fantastic and improbable architecture.
>
> Teachers and parents were intrigued and impressed by the way the boys and girls worked together; they hadn't reached the age when individuality takes precedence over collaboration. They visited and celebrated each other's contribution to the city, shared stories about its creation and where it came from in their lives, and we could only stand back and watch this miracle unfold. It was obvious that it was nothing but pure play; there was no thought of making art, only the absorption in the creative process. What could be more fun than playing in the dirt for hours?
>
> At some point they decided that the city was complete, and we asked them to pose for a few photographs as they stood behind their creation. It was about this time that a teacher shouted "LUNCH" and the children ran towards the cafeteria, destroying most of the city as they heeded the call.
>
> The adults were stunned, and as the students ate their sandwiches and talked about the city, it was obvious that their world expanded when lunch was called. It was refreshing to see that they could just move on. The features of play, joy, and especially irreverence were present everywhere in this experience. Baleskar (2007) explains, "If you ask the child, 'Why did you take the trouble to build it, and now you have destroyed it?' the child will not understand your question; but if you insist he will say, 'I built the castle because I liked to build it. I destroyed the castle because I liked to destroy it'" (p. 85). Such is the nature of childhood!

Let's go into this activity in more detail and let the children be our guides; this way we can better understand the workings of the topics contained in this chapter.

As the children created their world they formed it around conversations. They talked incessantly as they worked, negotiating with each other as someone's fence ran into someone else's garden, or a lake became part of a house. Or there might be conversations that had nothing to do with the project per se, but more to do with the social life of the group. All this contrasts with the traditional stereotype of the artist as a solitary figure, asocial and neurotic, and gives us another more democratic view of the creative process, one that is grounded in shared experiences.

An art class that David taught as part of the Masters program at California State University, San Bernardino, illustrates how the collaborative nature of art can build community through play and interaction:

> The students, who were mostly high school teachers, were asked to trace each other as they lay on the ground and then explore in color and texture the intersections of the silhouettes. Being on the ground, some lying, some sitting, already dissolved barriers that exist when we are separated by furniture and concepts. There is also literally something grounding about being on the floor.
>
> But it was the conversations that happened around the drawing that were so fascinating and revealing. They were able to process their frustrations with the educational system and come up with alternatives in their own teaching. Somehow the context of the group and the group activity freed their perception that learning requires a singular focus. On the contrary, as this exercise showed, it is in the interactions that learning takes place, interaction around a shared activity, in this case art.

The students involved in this playful collaborative project made all kinds of intellectual connections related to their teaching through secondary or peripheral conversations that took place naturally as they worked on their project collaboratively. Cloninger (2004) supports the importance of secondary or peripheral activities in fostering insight and the retention of information: "New research is suggesting that a wandering mind may be a good thing for humanity. A wandering mind appears to be a time when our brains are not 'doing' but rather 'being' and in that state (called a default brain state) we see an increase in self-awareness. By that I mean we have greater intuitive understanding of 'who we are' in relation to our bodies, thoughts, feelings and actions, to others and the universe at large" (p. 85).

The kind of environment used in learning is really important for what happens. When the kindergarten students played in the dirt it was a change of context for them, both physically and emotionally, that enlivened their experience and their perception of the world.

A sense of play and imitation can be observed in all young children, especially as we have slowly taken this away and many kindergarten classrooms have become focused more exclusively on academics. Wilson (2007) notes that "what children most need is a time and a place to play. . . . it is through play that they develop a sense of competence and make valuable discoveries about their social, cultural and physical environments" (p. 2).

Environments can also be limiting when our thinking becomes institutionalized; we take on a disembodied identity in relation to them. None of this was present when the kids built their city, or the graduate students drew and talked on the floor, or when the high school students chatted and drew themselves in text. What was present was playful creativity, community, and an open, adaptive, and emergent system where the context was the art. These qualities are enhanced when we go outside.

DREAMPLAY AND THE OUTSIDE

When David was a young boy living in a small village in England, the school curriculum consisted mostly of knitting, gardening, and nature walks. These nature walks would last for hours. The students spent a lot of time playing various games instead of identifying birds eggs or tracking the evolution of a frog; but these walks made an indelible impression on him and sowed the seeds of an appreciation of the outdoors that has persisted and grown throughout his life.

One of the most memorable aspects of these walks was when the students were able to dreamplay, laugh, and wander freely within a safe natural environment. The students entered a world of fancy, a world of lucid meandering that could be explored with creative abandon. There is an innate joy that develops from using imagination in this way.

Robinson (2011) has observed that all humans have creative capacity but by late adolescence a great percentage of this capacity has been lost. He sees this creative decline as a direct result of limited educational environments that restrain the natural human inclination to imagine, play, and engage in imaginative wonder.

As education becomes increasingly focused on the rational and directive, we lose sight of the importance of dreaming and especially dreaming in nature. It seems that we crave the deep space of outdoors more than ever; and as society becomes more and more preoccupied with virtual reality we need the tangible and unpredictable physicality of natural phenomena (Louv, 2012). In natural environments our senses come alive, almost as if we are returning to a place that is part of our being.

This is why we hold retreats in the San Jacinto wilderness as part of our MA program. The reason we like that environment so much (apart from its natural beauty and the magnificent ponderosa pines in the meadow) is that it allows students and teachers to break free of the constraints of human-made environments. Louv writes that "natural environments may also encourage introspection and may provide a psychological safe haven from the man-made pressures of society" (p. 14). When humans are immersed in the forces of nature there is a suspension of control.

We have witnessed this time and time again when students in the MA program discover themselves creatively as they build a shrine from natural materials, create a ritual circle together in the forest, or share their lives around a campfire. The authors' experience has confirmed that when students engage in environments and activities that open them to imagination, self-inquiry, and playful exploration they begin to embrace their creativity. Emergence happens more naturally in these kinds of settings. The patterns of relationship, interaction, process, participation, engagement, choice, and iterations become clearly observable. Emergent teaching relies on making use of these elements.

HEAD, BODY, AND LEGS

When the children built a city in the dirt, there was interactive play and they "played off" each other in ways that created a dynamic synergy. We call this kind of collaboration "interplay." A vivid and somewhat unusual example of this occurred in a sculpture class a few years ago when the students were asked to create a collaborative piece around an object. These shorter assignments are given to break up the longer ones that can last for a whole year. They often don't have a clear outcome but instead are allowed to evolve.

The unpredictable nature of this kind of interactive art has all the characteristics of emergent play. David calls this activity Head, Body, and Legs because each participative segment adds substance to the final outcome.

> The assignment was set up like a relay and the student who volunteered to start the process chose an object and then invited the next student to creatively extrapolate. The object was an orange.
>
> The first student peeled the orange in equal segments with a knife, and laid out the peel around the pulp like the petals of a flower.
>
> The second student took the center of the orange smeared the juice on her hand and used it as an adhesive for the peel which she then divided into tiny pieces which looked like fish scales.
>
> The third student separated the pulpy matter from the rest of the juice without destroying it so that it looked like a membrane and then stretched it out on the ground using toothpicks.
>
> The fourth student collected the pips from the orange and put them between her fingers and toes and then removed them with her mouth and spat them in to the stretched-out membrane.
>
> The last student collected all the components and mixed them with dirt and water and then smeared the mixture on the forehead of the other students and then herself.

This is a compelling example of interplay and as it evolved it included strong elements of performance art and ritual. The materials were not what we associate with the traditional stuff of art and the methods are also different from traditional art practices. No one claimed ownership of the piece; in fact, the last student's gesture of putting the mixture on everybody was a clear demonstration that it was a communal act. When others "possess" your art, it is almost as if they become part of your creative self.

The concept of interplay and the creative symbiosis that comes out of it can be adapted to other modalities and subject areas. For example, writing relays that develop into a collective stream of consciousness become literary versions of Heads, Bodies, and Legs where the student is not perceptually aware of how his part relates to the one that came before because all he is given is two lines or a word.

In elementary classes one can show a picture or art print and have students imagine what lies outside the border of the print in that nonexistent area of mystery. It is amazing to hear students play with different possibilities and either draw or write out their imaginary descriptions.

An alternative to this is to present students with a phrase or social convention that is taken for granted, such as the phrase "It's raining cats and dogs" or the use of high-heeled shoes, and have them explore their origins. Such playful activities and assignments create immediate interplay and joyful engagement. These are all experiments in emergence—emergence comes from the interplay of forces that create their own dynamic.

IRREVERENCE AND RUNNING AWAY

> Thus I spoke to him, and when he set out I entered the deep and savage way.
> —Dante

Many of the most influential thinkers in history questioned the prevailing authority. Although we educators often find this kind of questioning threatening, this questioning can be a sign of engagement. Sometimes it is helpful to reframe what otherwise feels like a lack of respect, see it as process, and engage with its energy.

The following story exemplifies how irreverence and defiance can lead to emergent possibilities that were unpredictable. It occurred in a setting where there was no intended implementation of these ideas, but what David experienced contained many of the themes of this book:

> I had had no instruction manual on how to teach when I started my first week in an advanced drawing class of 22 seniors in a small studio. In a way I was at an advantage on that first day, in that I didn't have a lot of preconceptions about teaching. I was naively expecting the students to follow the classroom

plan that I had spent most of the summer preparing, but it soon became apparent that there was much more going on in the classroom than I could predict or contain with a carefully crafted syllabus.

Previously, there had not been a great deal of student involvement in this class. Most of the students were seniors, many from Asia, and all were in the process of completing their college applications. Looking back, given this set of conditions and the content of the first assignment I had just given the students, it should not have been too surprising when there was a collective meltdown in which one student suddenly and without warning ran out of the classroom shouting, "I can't do this, I can't do this anymore." At this moment I seriously began to question my career choice, but I soon realized that the assignment had something to do with the meltdown.

At the time I was practicing formal Zen Buddhism and thought that the teachings contained universal truths that could be applied in all circumstances, to all people at all times, and I concluded that these students were ready to receive it. The assignment asked the question "Who am I?" and attempted to find the answer through a series of self-portraits. Given that for most of them their self-worth was being seriously questioned through the process of college applications, it is not surprising that many of them had such a severe reaction to the assignment. The implication was that their validity as person was being questioned. Now I was faced with a dilemma whether to be a disciplinarian or somehow stay with what was unfolding. My instincts told me to inhabit this space of uncertainty.

What is beautiful and ironic about this story as it evolves is that although it had all the appearances of a teacher's nightmare, it led to a dramatic shift in the classroom dynamics. David's responsibility as a teacher gave him no alternative but to deal with the repercussions of this event and really ask the question "Who am I?" of *himself.* The story continues:

> The meltdown was what I needed to get real, and what the students needed as a release. This is not something that could have been predicted, and it definitely was not in the lesson plan, but as is true of many of the best moments in teaching it's very unpredictability is what gives it vitality and eventually meaning.
>
> The student who ran out of the classroom came back and I took the opportunity to discuss what happened with the whole class. I became aware of all the pressures they were under and how the assignment made them question themselves even more. We spent time reframing how the assignment related to the course of study, but I also decided to put it on hold and instead help them with their college applications.
>
> I now had a relationship with the students based on trust and understanding. The defiant student, in engaging with the assignment, realized his deep desire to be of service to others. He went on to become one of the top graduating seniors and received a full scholarship to the Boston Museum School.
>
> But what is more important in the bigger picture of emergence over time is that the student eventually felt that being an artist was too narrow for him and he wanted to do something that more directly contributed to people's welfare;

so after he graduated from college he trained to be a nurse, and eventually intends to be a doctor. The defiant exit of the classroom and the subsequent immersion into the assignment of "Who Am I" planted the seeds for continued self-discovery.

This story points to something that is often forgotten: We teachers can too easily ignore the lives of our students outside the classroom as we push them to fulfill the demands of the curriculum and the mandates of society. Here David chose to incorporate his student's concerns and placed the emphasis on their lives and his relationship with them. This opened a space of authenticity where students were free to express themselves and discover their own passions.

This sense of discovery and passion spilled over to the student who left the classroom. He discovered a relationship between his identity as an artist and his passionate need to help others. Society stereotypically depicts the life of an artist as unconventional and that of a nurse as more socially acceptable, but that is because we probably have a narrow definition of both. When David asked his ex-student why he gave up art, he replied that he hadn't and that he practices his art as a nurse. For this student there was division, no separation in his identity.

If the student hadn't chosen the path of transgression and run out of the studio that day, what occurred subsequently may not have been possible. It took that act of defiance for him to define his life, and this is why "creative dissent" is important in the context of true learning. This story is particularly relevant to the life of teenagers who are looking for a context in which to experiment and discover themselves; perhaps our job as teachers and mentors is to provide that context by understanding the dynamics of emergence and the open possibilities that are put into play.

This story had a profound effect on David's teaching. He realized that intuitive cues are important indicators of emergence, that the larger arc of process is more significant than the prescribed lesson plan, that irreverence and play are important factors in a healthy classroom environment, and that this can be realized through authentic dialogue and the alchemy of time. He also understood why certain mentors had such a lasting and profound effect on him: they all exhibited these same qualities.

CONVERSING WITH SHEEP

Those having torches will pass them on to others.
—Plato, *The Republic*

It can be tempting to narrowly keep to the science of emergence. But when the metaphor is loosened, the idea of something "emerging" is close to each one of us. This is especially true when one considers the direction of their life and the ways their life has *emerged* to where it is. These next stories and narratives bring us back to the positive influence that teachers and mentors can have in the lives of their students—of "a life unfolding." In these stories, look for examples of playful eccentricity, joyful independence, and creative defiance or irreverence.

Mr. Oaks was David's art teacher in high school. He had a huge red beard and booming voice and dedicated his life to eliminating overhead power lines in his town. He often stayed after class to help David with his drawing or to experiment with abstractions. His mentoring and his ability to step outside of the norm was the germ of David's passion for art.

Then there was Rev. Saxton, the vicar of West Farleigh Church in Kent, England, who had a poetic and creative instinct that didn't necessarily conform to the church teachings and was at its best when he stepped outside its doctrinal confines. David remembers riding his bike to church early one Sunday to ring the bells, to find Rev. Saxton standing in the middle of a field talking to a flock of sheep. And what was most amazing to this young boy is that the sheep seemed to be gazing at him in rapt attention.

Whether Rev. Saxton saw the sheep symbolically as Christ saw them or he was actually conversing with them didn't really matter to David because as a young boy he was intensely curious about the nature of existence and God. So imagine his relief to see this pillar of the church conversing with a flock of sheep and presenting another, contrary reality to the traditional Church procedures.

This reality is implied in Whitehead's ironic statement "to a learned man, matter exists in test tubes, animals in cages, art in museums, religion in churches, knowledge in libraries." Whitehead, instead, saw real learning as uncontained, imaginative, and related to actual experience. This is best exemplified in the trickster, a figure in the mythology of many cultures whose function is to break the rules of the gods or nature, sometimes maliciously, but ultimately with positive effects.

Hyde (2010) puts it this way: "I want to argue a paradox that the myth asserts; that the origins, liveliness, and durability of cultures require that there be space for figures whose function is to uncover and disrupt the very things the culture is based on." For David, Mr. Oaks and the Rev. Saxton were examples of mentors who playfully bent tradition and who were not afraid of irreverence.

The kindergarten kids who ran across their city and the student who stormed out of the room also fulfilled this function of irreverence and defiance. It seems that if we embrace this trickster figure in our students and ourselves and see it as an integral part of the landscape of emergence, then it provides an important counterbalance to the mechanistic and limiting dynamics of the classroom and society at large.

The Rev. Saxton had an occupation and sensibilities similar to the groundbreaking poet Gerard Manley Hopkins, whose poem "Pied Beauty" wonderfully encapsulates the spirit and bewilderment of God as trickster:

> Glory be to God for dappled things—
> For skies of couple-colour as a brinded cow;
> For rose-moles all in stipple upon trout that swim;
> Fresh-firecoal chestnut-falls; finches' wings;
> Landscape plotted and pieced—fold fallow, and plough;
> And all trades, their gear and tackle trim.
> All things counter, original, spare, strange;
> Whatever is fickle, freckled (who knows how?)
> With swift, slow; sweet, sour; adazzle, dim;
> He fathers-forth whose beauty is past change:
> Praise Him.

bell hooks (1994), in writing about teaching in colleges and universities, emphasizes among other things the vital connection between joy, excitement, and a learning process that is emergent.

> To enter classroom settings in colleges and universities with the will to share the desire to encourage excitement was to transgress. Not only did it require movement beyond accepted boundaries, but excitement could not be generated without a full recognition of the fact that there could never be an absolute set agenda governing teaching practices. Agendas had to be flexible, had to allow for spontaneous shifts in direction. . . . this excitement could co-exist with and even stimulate intellectual and/or academic engagement. (p. 7)

As we have seen in many of the examples cited in this chapter, transformations that occur when we fully embrace emergence are often precipitated through an act of transgression.

As hooks points out this can be something as innocent as excitement or as radical as running out of the classroom. Either way, acts like these create the space for emergence and help bring about real change.

Chapter Six

Creativity

The Ceaseless Imperative

While establishing a playful state of mind is essential for optimal performance, the underlying impetus for joyful play is creativity. Creativity from the perspective of emergence is not ancillary to learning but integral to it; neither is it limited by particular art forms. Creativity is an imperative that is encoded into our being and is inherent to the natural world. One could say that emergence is creativity in action.

Unfortunately, in the current educational environment, this important aspect of learning has been marginalized in the clamor for testing. Art classes, music, dance, and performance have all been relegated to the electives in our schools, and even the humanities are seen as less relevant than the sciences. One way to redress this imbalance is not only to bring back the arts and humanities into our educational landscape but more importantly to affirm the creative intelligence that underlies all disciplines.

As a society we talk about creativity in very general terms, but creativity has its own set of internal patterns and indicators. This chapter will look at creativity in relation to complexity and emergence and provide ways in which this understanding can help teachers and students have a more fulfilling and significant educational experience. It also contains stories that illustrate how creative engagement and insight have inspired learning.

In David's own childhood he experienced this firsthand, and in a way this became the basis for his passion for arts education:

I found out that I wanted to be an artist when I was 13 and immediately asked my father if I could follow this instinct and go to an art school. My father declined because he wanted me to have a safer career. But the imperative was too strong to ignore, so I kept asking until he relented. Immediately my grades in the rest of my classes improved dramatically.

Not only did this story underscore the importance of creativity in the general context of learning, but it also had the added benefit of reawakening my father's creativity. Unknown to me he had been an avid painter earlier in his life. He now felt he had permission to share his love of art.

This story is not unlike much of the research that links arts and creativity with cognitive achievement:

When the arts are integrated with instruction in other content areas, such math or science, that other content area is learned more efficiently. . . . learners achieve a deeper understanding, acquire an ability to think more flexibly using content knowledge, and develop enhanced critical thinking and creativity. (Sawyer, 2012, p. 391)

We have seen the benefits of various arts in their own teaching and feel there are preliminary understandings that can help integrate the arts and learning. Since most educators are not trained in a specific art form, it helps when they get past negative messages and stereotypes about their ability to be creative and teach creatively.

UNDOING NEGATIVE MESSAGES ON CREATIVITY

Many attitudes about creativity come from how culture defines it. Just as in much of institutionalized religion, access to God (and the art, music, and literature that describes "Him") is mediated through religious institutions and architecture, in a similar way art has become the province of galleries, museums, and critics and appears to require a specialized knowledge and vocabulary to understand it. As a result many people feel they are excluded from this world and by implication the creative process. More specifically they are conditioned to think that they are not artists and do not have the necessary creative instincts and skills.

This is compounded by the negative input that many teachers and parents give to children, especially in their formative years, which then becomes generational. Because in many people's minds creativity is associated with specific art forms (and the skill sets that are required for mastery), if they are excluded from these forms then they assume that they lack a more general understanding of creativity and its scope. For many students the negative impact of this conditioning is that it limits other forms of creative expression in their lives and in the classroom.

So how can educators and students come to embrace the idea of creativity as accessible to all? One way is to look at the conditioning that prevents us from accessing our natural creativity. Who was it that told us we couldn't draw or play the piano or dance or that we're dumb? And how deeply was that embedded in our psyche when we heard it, so that it reemerged every time we were faced with a blank sheet of paper or the keys of a piano? These are devastating messages for a young child to hear, and undoing them can be difficult but, as we shall describe, ultimately freeing. It could be said that until we as educators practice this in our own lives we will be unable to teach creatively in a way that invites complexity and emergence in to the class-room.

Feeling separate from one's innate creativity can have a profound effect at an emotional and psychological level; there is a feeling of alienation and numbness. In a different context, Macy et al. describe what this sense of separation can feel like. She writes of our loss of connection with the natural world: "Last night we shared stories from our experiences which awakened our concern—even anguish—over what is happening to the natural world in our time . . . it has called us to experiment with new ways of healing our separation from nature" (Seed et al., 2007, pp. 79–80). They use the words *concern* and *anguish* to describe this separation. Not recognizing our innate creativity can be felt in similar ways but often at an unconscious level.

On the other hand the transformation that occurs when one traverses this imagined separation reveals a way of being that is fully engaged and fully alive. We say *imagined separation* because as humans we are never apart from this creative force. This imaginary separation is another part of our conditioning and it slowly calcifies as we get older. We saw in an earlier chapter where the kindergartners were building their city the creative impera-tive being actualized.

For young children creativity is full immersion in process and the unfold-ing of possibility. These possibilities happen in the space of complexity. In this space the children are unfettered and objects and occasions take on a multitude of meanings. By observing this process we can also learn to see past our conditioned reality into a world that is luminous and present.

Conditioned reality is represented by Magritte's well-known painting of a pipe, *Ceci n'est pas une pipe*" in which he points out the delusional nature of perception. The important lesson here is that we often accept our condition-ing as reality, and the function of transformative education is to see past these conditionings to access our innate creativity.

John Berger (1977) in his book *Ways of Seeing* gives a very lucid exam-ple of how cultural and aesthetic conditioning can influence how we view the world. In the example he cites critiques of the Frans Hals painting *Regentess-es of the Old Men's Almshouse* by well-known art historians and points out that the language they use is riddled with clichés, borrowed concepts, and mystification, which in his view prevent us from seeing the psychological drama that is unfolding in the painting and what actually makes it great. He observes, "when an image is presented as a work of art, the way people look at it is affected by a whole series of learnt assumptions. . . . many of these assumptions no longer accord with the world as it is (The world as-it-is is more than pure objective fact, it includes consciousness)." And again: "Out of true with the present, these assumptions obscure the past. They mystify rather than clarify. . . . Mystification is the process which explains away what might otherwise be evident" (pp. 11–15).

Berger's observations about art also apply to the ways all of us are conditioned by learned assumptions about creativity. Once art is demystified it is the beginning of a process of democratization, which affirms a deeper creativity that is accessible to us all. In our graduate classes in holistic education students confront their conditioned responses to what they think art and creativity have to mean.

As physicists Bohm and Peat (1997) assert, "Creativity, in almost every area of life, is blocked by a wide range of assumptions that are taken for granted by society as a whole" (p. 235). When this is understood and integrated, students begin to act creatively with fewer predisposed assumptions about their inability as artists.

Another mistaken assumption is that art has ineffable qualities that are not accessible to most of us, and because it can't be understood, it can't be critiqued. Kirshenblatt-Gimblett (1998) observes that our society conditions us to believe that "standards are absolute and not relative . . . that they are inherent, that they are not culturally or historically determined" (p. 425). But she goes on to argue that all of that is "an architecture to sustain the status quo" (p. 425). One could argue that this applies not only to art but to education as well.

In our masters' program these insights are used to undo habitual thinking, unexamined cultural norms, and the obscure language that surrounds them. This deconstructive process functions as a way of clearing the ground for emergence, like weeding and preparing a seedbed before planting. We have found that without these preliminary steps our students do not experience the same creative release, or the integration that comes out of it.

THE DYNAMICS OF CREATIVITY

To continue the analogy of a seedbed, one of the most effective ways of preserving soil fertility is to leave it fallow and unused for a period of time. We see the same dynamic in creativity. When students have examined and understood the conditions that prevent them from fulfilling their creative potential it is often followed by a period of fallowness. Just like seeds lying dormant in winter, students need time for new ideas to lie silent and unhurried. This is a necessary precondition for creative emergence. A space is being created that allows new ideas and visions to gestate and emerge.

In the classroom setting this period of fallowness can be disconcerting, because none of the normal indicators of progress are present. But that appearance might be societies' and our own predispositions, which are focused on goals and often confuse indolence with natural rest and the regeneration that can come out of it.

This brings up another important aspect of the creative process: the concept of "no time." Rather than seeing unused time as antithetical to learning, we could shift our thinking and make space for it, so that the creative imperative is activated. A germinating seed, once it splits open through the action of water, soil, and darkness, has a momentum that is irrepressible. Likewise creativity blossoms, and at this point it goes beyond analogy and becomes a reflection of our relation with an expanding universe. This is something that we all share, a universal and irresistible force, an imperative.

As we saw earlier, Indra's Net describes nonseparation in terms of millions of jeweled nodes reflecting every other jeweled node. We pointed out that this has parallels with quantum mechanics and a nodal view of space (Wolfram, 2010). Bell's theorem and subsequent experimental evidence also support the notion of nonlocality in which spatially separated events cannot be considered as independent happenings but rather as inherently connected. Creativity is built into the fabric of the universe and the creative impulse is as much a part of us as is the new star system being born in the dream-time of space.

The image of Indra's Net would not be nearly as compelling, and its description of the universe not as convincing, if it were contained by a static view of infinity. Just like Magritte's pipe the word *infinite* could easily become a conceptual construct if weren't for the fact that each node is infinitely reflected in each other node and inherently emergent. It has no definable limits, is undulating and expanding.

Kauffman (2010) in his groundbreaking book *Reinventing the Sacred* explains that "we live in a universe, biosphere, and human culture, that is not only emergent but radically creative . . . this is a central part of the new scientific worldview" (p. 5). Kauffman deliberately makes a connection between human culture (our histories, inventions, ideas, and actions), the universe, and the creative imperative that animates them both. This notion of "imperative" depicts a capacity that cannot be deliberately resisted or unacknowledged; and when it is allowed to be expressed, it has much more the feeling of mutual dependence and complexity, like the matrix of Indra's Net.

The creative imperative is lived out in our daily lives. It is always operating; it is not just a state of mind. We are an integral part of a cosmic creative process that is infinite, dynamic, and ceaseless. A cyclical process in which birth, death, and renewal is a part of every event. In much the same way, when we engage in the creative process we reenact this cosmic cycle.

And just like the evolving universe, creativity is not an exclusive transformative event but occurs again and again. If we embrace creativity in this way we feel a part of something larger than ourselves, a process that is at the very root of our being.

LINDA'S STORY

One beautiful example of the dynamics of creative emergence occurred in one of David's classes. It speaks to this broader perspective of creativity:

> David gave his drawing students an assignment dealing with personal history and specifically how it is reflected in architectural space and the objects that it contains. Linda had already collected photographic images of her childhood room and her favorite things and transferred them on to a large piece of paper using acetone. Now she was attempting to connect the images with drawing, but it seemed like a contrived formal device; the dynamics of the composition were out of balance.
>
> David asked her what she was thinking about and what she was trying to convey. She replied that when she was home she loved to stare out of the window and that is why she put the large rectangle on the upper left hand corner of the drawing. Somehow, though, this image lacked resolution, so David asked her what other associations the window had for her.
>
> She replied that it represented a portal into another world of the imagination, but then added that her mother had always insisted that she should have curtains but Linda had not wanted them. This had been a cause of contention between the two of them. Linda added that this kind of thing did not seem to be a legitimate basis for art. It presented her with a dilemma, and she left the class that evening frustrated.
>
> When she first attempted to resolve the spatial imbalance and drew the window she was still operating under the conditions of her formal training; but because of her need to go beyond objective representation she was not satisfied. It did not convey the emotional intensity that she wanted. She still felt she could resolve it technically but she couldn't, and that is when she was asked what associations the window had for her. She didn't know and tried to deflect the question by saying this was not the purview of art.
>
> Also she felt intense pressure because the assignment was due at the end of class and she had never been late before. She was a straight-A student who had very high standards for herself. David decided to extend the deadline for her. After a few days she announced she had resolved the dilemma: she would include the curtains but they would be pulled back from the window. And she e-mailed her mother and asked her to describe all the reasons why she insisted

that Linda have curtains. Linda transferred the words from her mother's response onto the curtains in her drawing and it immediately resolved the formal and emotional issues.

Let's look at this story in the context of creative emergence. Linda had a lot of technical ability; this had been apparent in her previous assignments. But this was not enough. At some level she was looking for a deeper connection with the creative process. The new assignment provided her with that opportunity. David could have insisted that she complete it by the assigned date or suffer the consequences, but he would have missed an important opportunity for creative emergence; he saw that she was not shirking responsibility but rather was trying to resolve a creative dilemma.

As teachers we are either fearful of or hostage to time and don't allow for that period of "unused time" and gestation to occur. This took place in the three days that lapsed between classes, and the resolution came out of the stark reality of Linda's dilemma. And what a beautiful resolution it was. Not only did it resolve the formal aspects of the drawing, but it also resolved a contentious aspect of her relationship with her mother: she was able to present her own needs and her mother's preferences together in the neutral architecture of the drawing.

We see the important role of the teacher in this resolution. David needed to enter that space of not knowing that often precedes transformation. If he had insisted that the drawing be finished by the end of class, or seen creativity only in terms of technical ability, then an opportunity would have been lost and none of the resolution would have taken place.

The creative process inheres not just in art but in all things and contains dilemmas that are often both personal and technical. Doubt and uncertainty are part of the landscape of the creative process. This is important for all of us teachers to realize, no matter what our discipline. The creative process in many ways replicates the principles of chaos, complexity, and emergence. It is a window into emergent teaching.

We also see in this example how important dialogue is as a way of unlocking creativity. If Linda had not stepped outside her comfort zone and had she kept her thoughts and feelings to herself, not sharing them with David or her mother, then this wonderful resolution would not have occurred. And if she had not been prepared to "go it alone" in that three-day period of reflection and "not knowing," then again none of this would have happened. This interplay of reflective solitude and dialogue is crucial to the dynamics of creativity and something that is not generally recognized as important in education, where the emphasis is on the quickest delivery and regurgitation of information.

CREATIVITY IN THE CLASSROOM

What actually happens during this period of creative gestation, and how do we orient ourselves to it as teachers? Helping students navigate this period of uncertainty requires an understanding that in practice emergence is situated within individual circumstances and personal histories, and the unfolding of creative expression is not predictable or uniform. Although set periods of reflection are important in the classroom, as teachers we should be aware of individual students' needs to process information in "no time" and find their own path of creative emergence.

This often occurs outside the classroom as it did with Linda. "No time" also applies to teachers where we can hold and process this ambiguity. Uncertainty is rooted in questions, and these questions cannot be fully addressed in the context of a classroom; teachers need to get away both mentally and physically.

Realizing this need for renewal in our work with graduate students, we have often emphasized the importance of retreat. The retreat environment gives time and space to address personal and professional questions of uncertainty and inner conflict. Retreat allows access to one's innate creativity and invites resolution. "Retreat" does not have to be a formal event that is group-oriented; often it can be an informal space of alone time where creative emergence can take its natural course.

Resolution can also occur in group settings, and the exchange of ideas and "creative dissent" that happens in a group can unlock our creative potential. Lehrer (2012) addresses this notion of creative dissent in this way: "We naturally assume . . . that negative feedback stifles the sensitive imagination. But it turns out we're tougher than we thought. The imagination is not meek—it doesn't wilt in the face of conflict. Instead it is drawn out, pulled from its usual hiding place" (p. 161). He contrasts this process with brainstorming, which he feels is an ineffective way of unlocking creativity because it is based on consent, and creativity needs a "disturbed" environment (like a field that is tilled) for it to be realized.

David remembers his time in graduate school, which was a period of intense creativity, mostly because there was an opportunity for creative dissent and discussion between students and professors. This took place in a formal studio setting but more importantly it carried over to the informal social environment of the campus and the White Hart pub.

The students also put up a large white board where they were invited to present their ideas. This initiated a dialogue which in itself became the basis for critiques and also a collaborative installation. To establish an informal atmosphere where dialogue and critical exchange can occur, Sam has created periodic "coffee houses" where muffins and refreshments are served and where students share and critique their work.

Critique, as dialogue and feedback, is not a summative evaluation or criticism; rather it provides creative exchange. Robinson (2011) addresses this point: "At the right time in the right way, critical appraisal is essential. At the wrong time it can kill an emerging idea" (p. 155). This is important. There needs to be "rules of engagement" that maintain civility.

Emergent teaching is not something that we own as a method. It doesn't follow egocentric preferences for outcome but is determined by a larger collective symbiosis and the expansive nature of the creative process.

For critical dialogue to operate with vitality and integrity there needs to be a balance between criticism and praise, and this is where the role of the teacher is essential. She is often the arbiter of this balance and can interject whenever she feels there is an overemphasis on the negative or too much praise. This takes practice; it is not something one can learn in a theoretical setting, and then apply verbatim to the classroom; there will be mistakes along the way.

Not only in the area of critique but in any context of emergent teaching, the fear of mistakes should not keep one from pursuing a new idea. One of the travesties of modern education is that mistakes are increasingly viewed as terminal, so as teachers we are afraid to make them, and the practice of teaching is diminished by fear—the antithesis of creative emergence.

Again, Robinson observes that "if you're not prepared to make mistakes, it's unlikely that you'll come up with anything original" (p. 153). From a perspective of emergence, mistakes have energy locked in them, and seeing them as integral to the creative process unlocks that energy. Yo-Yo Ma once said, "I welcome the first mistake. Because then I can shrug it off and keep smiling. Then I can get on with the performance and turn off the part of the mind that judges everything. . . . it's when I'm least conscious of what I'm doing, when I'm lost in the emotion of the music, that I'm performing at my best" (in Lehrer, pp. 88–89). This leads to the larger question of what elements energize the creative process.

INCONGRUITY AND CREATIVITY

The things we fear most in organizations—fluctuations, disturbances, imbalances—are the primary sources of creativity.
—Margaret J. Wheatley

We are persuaded by culture that there is a certain immutable order that underlies and determines our existence. This often is reflected by a "fixed identity" that can limit the experience of the vitality and evanescence of life, especially when it determines one's life path so that one is constantly repeating behaviors, which eventually form a monolithic, often intransigent identity.

One of the principles of emergence is that life is not predictable—that forces, in the cosmic sense, are not guided by our preferences for outcome. So the function of the creative imperative and emergence is to call these assumptions about a solid identity into question. One way of doing this is to deliberately bring forces and elements together that are incongruous.

What if identity was viewed as multifaceted, fluctuating, and full of contradictions, and what if this could be expressed in ways that combined different disciplines? Emergence builds upon openness and layered complexity. When students are encouraged to bring these qualities to a creative project or long-term inquiry, this adds a natural complexity to the process. The following is an example of how multifaceted identity is, and how this awareness can deepen creative expression:

> The students created a self-portrait and reversed the usual sequence for figure drawing, which is to draw the outline and then fill it in. Seen in the context of life paths, this approach mirrors the philosophical basis for predetermination that we described earlier, which as we saw, limits the possibilities for emergence. The alternative is to work from the inside out so that the usual orientation points are not accessible. This opens up a kaleidoscope of relationships and possibilities that are not accessible with predetermined boundaries.
>
> Because the drawing developed from the interior, and the students used different mediums and sources, the perimeter of the drawing followed the dictates of those choices and was not a literal representation of the person. As a result their perceptions of identity were more fluid, interactive, and emergent.
>
> The sources they drew from to create their self-portrait included text, and it became the medium that formed most of the image. This text could simply be thoughts the artist was having as the work was being created, or descriptions of their psychophysical and sociocultural identity; it could also include autobiographical elements in the form of letters or diaries. These were combined with anatomical drawings of different parts of the body, actual imprints of skin and hair, or even X-ray images.
>
> As is clear from the description of the process, the students were free to play with many different and seemingly contradictory elements, all held within the context of self-identity. They took great joy in exploring this new paradigm, as if they were exploring a range of possibilities in themselves. It was clear validation of the saying "I am multitudes" and the imperative that drives this expression of emergence.

When one is able to free oneself from unexamined assumptions and enter this unpredictable and emergent universe of incongruous juxtapositions, a very important aspect of creative emergence can be seen. There is an awareness that we don't possess a fixed identity, that humans are indeed made up of "multitudes," and as a result one is more able to accept the foibles of others and the vicissitudes of life.

This awareness is a journey and opens the way for a teacher to create an environment of acceptance. The students are invited to enter that field of "unknowing" and experience the creative release and confidence that emerges. They find an internal authority rather than relying on an imposed obligation. A bond is created between teacher and student that is defined by risk-taking and the power of creative emergence. The result is a shared commitment to creative learning.

As we can see with these examples, creative emergence and the imperative that animates it do not follow a smooth or predictable path. In fact, as we have found out, its very unpredictability is what gives it vitality. But we have also found out that to understand this on an intellectual level is very different from experiencing it in the classroom.

THE CEASELESS IMPERATIVE

In all the stories shared in this book where a creative outcome emerged and transformation resulted, there is a kind of urgency or "imperative" under the surface. It was inherent *in* the process rather than being an external element that was imposed. What was it that drove these students to seek so intently? In their seeking they were willing to risk their identities as well as a particular outcome; so there is something much more powerful at work here.

Perhaps this is part of an instinctual imperative that needs to be acknowledged. Humans are essentially creative beings, and it is this very creativity that animates and nurtures us. This undeniable urgency is innately human and cannot be contrived or imposed; it just needs opportunity. To not use this creative imperative in our teaching is to ignore a central element of who we are and what it could mean for an education that has real significance.

Chapter Seven

Aunt Kath Serves Tea

Ritual and Emergence

Rituals are an integral part of emergent teaching and provide a rich context for it. Rather than being hollow repetitions, they can create a safe environment for community to evolve, encourage imaginative play, and give us symbols and metaphors that relate to shifts in perception. In other words, they ground transformation in concrete events. Without these foci, the energy and creativity of emergence would become dissipated, and the participants would feel less empowered.

Rituals come in many forms, and they can add depth and meaning to life both in and out of the classroom. The following story from David is an example of a simple, accessible ritual, one that is inseparable from everyday life.

In the early eighties when I was fully immersed in formal Zen training, I visited my great aunt Kath who lived by herself in a small semi-detached house in a village in Kent, England, the same house where her mother was raised. I was living in America and it had been over ten years since I had visited Kath. She was in her late seventies and was fairly fragile and had to be careful lifting and carrying things.

After welcoming me to her home she invited me to sit at the kitchen table. The room was very sparse and probably little changed since the time her husband Len was alive. Many layers of cream paint covered the shelves and shelf brackets, and neatly folded pages of the *News Chronicle* were placed under one table leg to keep it from wobbling. All this was the setting for the making, serving, and drinking of tea. I had been introduced to tea ceremonies at the Zen Center and had taken tea from several tea masters. Aunt Kath was not familiar with this ritual or the traditions that formed it, but had been serving tea for most of her life, so there was naturalness to her actions. When she warmed the big, brown teapot she treated it like an old friend; the willow pattern teacups and saucers were arranged like an offering. She poured the tea with the relaxed attention that comes from doing it thousands of times, and when she carried the tea across the kitchen there was an overwhelming feeling that her attention was on her guest and how best to serve him.

The transition between the serving of tea, the conversations around it, and the cleaning up and putting away of the teapot, cups, and saucers was seamless, and I felt like I was taking the spirit of ritual with me as I said goodbye. This interaction and the ritual that surrounded it were made even more poignant by the fact that Aunt Kath passed away a few months later.

This everyday tradition of afternoon tea has particular characteristics that it shares in common with other rituals—at their best they evolve and are redefined by the participants. But what are the characteristics that make this a ritual activity, and what can we learn from it in connection with emergent teaching? Aunt Kath had carried out this ritual many times, reaching the point where she didn't really have to think about it and was able to animate the ritual and David through her un-self-conscious actions and service.

Seligmann et al. (2008) elaborate on the power of ritual as an interactive performance that accentuates communication and responsiveness. "The criterion for which actions from the past should become part of the ritual canon is simply based on whether a continued performance of them helps refine one's ability to respond to others" (p. 34). Ritual activity is different from routinized behavior in that it is infused with attention and purpose. Thus, it has a natural creativity embedded in the present, rather than being merely a routine embedded in the past. This awareness is rooted in a confirmation of the emotional and symbolic meaning of the ritual and seeing it as a way of fostering community.

Serving tea was a very important form of communication for Aunt Kath's generation; it created an atmosphere that transcends words. At the same time, because it is a stimulant, it is a medium that invites conversation. A tea set is called a service for other reasons than its function; it is an opportunity to serve others, and that is subtler than it appears.

Service in this context emphasizes a seeming paradox: pulling back while still orchestrating the movements of the ritual. This apparent contradiction is resolved when the objects, environment, and mediums become alive for the recipient. For Aunt Kath and David this was heightened by the simplicity of the room and her own humility.

We have found that one of the central criteria for emergent teaching is getting out of the way. In most educational systems it is assumed that results come from manipulating information or processes to fit a prescribed outcome. With emergence there is a shift in emphasis so that all the related systems become part of the gestalt of the event. In this case the serving of tea, the simplicity of the room, the form and color of the objects, their antiquity, and Aunt Kath's relationship with David all contributed to the richness of the experience and were held within the context as ritual. But without the component of service the ritual would have been lifeless and static.

As with traditional Asian tea ceremonies, certain actions give meaning and substance to ritual, and these have three foundational aspects that evolve and become seamless as the ritual becomes deeper. These are form, formality, and informality. These were all present in Aunt Kath's ritual, and, as we shall see, have different emphases depending on the nature of the ritual.

Form in this example is what makes a good cup of tea. There is a particular way of warming the teapot, pouring the water into it just before it boils, letting it steep for the right amount of time, and attending to the details of presentation. None of this is particularly specialized, but it does take practice and awareness.

Formality is practiced to keep the attention on the process. There is a dynamic tension however that is somewhat subtle and intuitive. Without enough formality, the presentation would become too subjective, and the spaciousness of the ritual would be diminished. With too much formality, actions become rigid, predictable, and self-conscious. So through practice a balance is reached. The result is a feeling of naturalness, ease, and presence, a focused *informality*. In essence, what the server is doing is creating space for the objects and environment to come alive together so that the participants can feel more fully present.

Presence is another facet of emergence that occurs more readily in a deliberately created ritual context, when all the participants have a common focus. For Kath and David this was the kitchen and the memories embedded in the physical environment. For a teacher it could be including the world of the students in the way the classroom is laid out, what is displayed on the walls, and how it represents the intersection of her life and the lives of her students.

In the more developed forms of ritual, there is an opportunity for informality and collaboration. Seligmann et al. (2008) note that "ritual was not some discreet realm of human action and interaction, set apart and distinct from other forms of human action. Instead we see it as a modality of human engagement with the world" (p. 10). In the classroom ritual can be used to deepen a sense of community and to create an environment of trust and safety where creative emergence can take place.

The following stories provide ways to explore the nature of *informality* as an important aspect of ritual. They also relate to a sense of place, in this case a wilderness retreat setting. A sense of place is important to ritual. It grounds it with texture and color and sound (Swimme and Tucker, 2011).

After a period of quiet the students were asked to go in to a forest with an open mind and discover a spot that had particular meaning for them. We left this activity open-ended because we feel that it takes time to understand the natural world at a more intimate level, and actually find one's place in it.

Once the students had settled on a locale, they were asked to build a simple piece of sculpture from found materials that represent their relationship with place. They were not given any specific instructions on how this structure should be built, or references that they could pull from; but as it developed the process had all the characteristics of ritual (imbuing objects and actions with personal significance) and reflected a need many of us have to create place and objects that are a symbolic focus for our lives.

After its completion the students returned, and, as with all activities, time was given for processing. The initial dialogue that took place in these meetings included words like *sacred, profound, moving, confusing, lonely.* Our job as facilitators was not to judge these responses but include them in the rich texture of the process. The layered nature of experience, collaborative dialogue, and communal sharing created strong conditions for emergence.

This had much in common with David's tea ritual with Aunt Kath in that various layered experiences were imbued with meaning and significance. Reflecting on this connection, it became apparent to the two of us that the building of shrines had moved into the landscape of ritual in that the students had signified their experience with symbolism and personal meaning that was communal in nature. (Ritual moves to a different level when it is shared with others.)

Also, there was a kind of consolidation or closure—a sanctifying of action—that occurred throughout this processing. David now created yet another layer of experience by having the students visit each other's shrines as a group. This was a time to further articulate and share, even ritualize, how their shrine connected them with place, their personal histories, and one another.

The shrines represented a place of retreat for each student, where they would return during the weekend to process further. An emotional space was created that they could take with them as they left the mountain to return to the city. In relation to art, the shrines reflected a growing confidence in a personal aesthetic that revealed the students' common connection with the natural world. Importantly, the two of us did not set out to create ritual; ritual emerged out of the symbolic meaning the students gave to the complex of experiences. By noticing this, we could enhance the significance of the event as ritual.

In the story above, the informal aspect of ritual was illustrated. The next narrative is a continuation of the shrine activity, but it shows a more formalized, deliberate use of ritual space. The activity was ritualized to unify personal and community experience:

The students were now ready to move on to creating a collaborative project in the form of a circle. A circle is a unifying symbol, which is found in many cultures and has emergent power because it is endless. Circles are used in many different ways in contemporary settings for community building, resolving conflict, celebration, and healing and support.

In our previous activities we introduced students to contemplation as a way of focusing and recognizing their relationship with the natural environment. Because contemplation is not limited to a single activity, we emphasized that the process of gathering materials was as important as the product itself.

This seamlessness of gathering, building, collaborating, and sharing formed an important bridge between the art and life. Understanding this connection imbued the processes with ritual meaning and a recognition that both we and the natural world are open systems. Given the heightened sensitivity to the surroundings and each other, it was not surprising that when poems were recited from a dwelling in the center of the circle they expressed in words and imagery a strong feeling of interconnectedness and emergence. This was also apparent in the reflection papers that the students wrote later.

The first student made a strong connection between ritual and creating community: "Ritual was important at the James' Reserve because it held us together as a solid community. . . . Play was also very important . . . it invited community building and cooperation. Both are very important for the classroom as they emphasize community and team building skills."

In the next two examples the ritual space provided an opportunity to make symbolic and metaphorical connections between the activity and the students' lives. One student narrates:

As I was breaking apart thin branches to represent the people who live within the earth, I was thinking about life. Suddenly my thoughts were with my eighteen-year-old cousin who passed away on March 2 of this year. His death made a big impact on my life. As I was thinking of him and how I wanted to include him in my piece of artwork, I came across a specific branch that had two thinner branches sticking out making it look like a cross. . . . At the end of the retreat I felt connected to that spot again because I felt as though it became my spot. I went back to it while I was looking for materials to build my section of the circle. It made me smile. It made me remember my cousin. It felt as though I left a piece of him there.

Another student:

The process brought to mind many linking thoughts, emotions, interconnections, and metaphors. The tour through the woods and building shrines was a perfect example of a postmodern teaching approach. The pristine forest reserve is a perfect learning environment for exploration, observation and understanding. . . . The beautiful natural circle that represented each one of us was an amazing communal activity that became an incredible, almost indescribable work of art. When we were building it, I felt that we were a village community and that we were hunting and gathering for the good of the community.

Yet another student discovered her innate creativity and how that imbued the activity with sacredness:

Life is Art! I do not believe there is a separation between the two. Real life is infused into the work and can be depicted in many ways, as we saw at the retreat. The choices, the patterns, the natural materials were all somehow connected to the finished work. It is the visual landscape of hopes and dreams, of love and loss. To be part of another's life, to be side by side in that process, to me, is sacred.

Finally, a humorous example of how the ritual and community are taken into the world:

This is a good path: I enjoyed the honesty above all. On the way home we stopped to get coffee at Starbucks. From here all the way home, we had ALL GREEN LIGHTS. Now that is something to wonder about! All red on the way up and all green on the way back.

These passages as a whole represent the next stage of ritual emergence: presenting one's insights to the community so that they can benefit from them. Just as Aunt Kath's serving of tea was enlivened by her sense of service, participating in ritual and sharing its significance with others becomes an act of altruism and generosity.

Next we will follow one student's personal ritual journey that developed the informal and innovative aspects of ritual in startling ways. In this story there is an expansion of ritual not only in the sense of more complex layers, but in the personal significance that was symbolized. These processes were transforming for the individual student and the whole community. As we shall see, the main protagonist in the story never stopped exploring the emergent possibilities of the ritual journey.

JONAH'S STORY: A HEALING JOURNEY OF RITUAL EMBODIMENT

After the disastrous and tragic events following Katrina in New Orleans, Idyllwild Arts Academy accepted several students from New Orleans Center for the Creative Arts (NOCCA). Among these students was a senior, Jonah, who became one of the most engaged, innovative, and caring students to come through the school.

Immediately after he arrived at the school he started to think of ways of processing his displacement from New Orleans through his art. It was obvious from his interest in the German artist Joseph Beuys that his approach would include aspects of ritual embodiment.

Beuys went against the prevailing aesthetic of the 1980s by presenting performance art that was provocative and sometimes disruptive. His performance piece "Conversations with a Rabbit" is particularly significant in this context. In it he covered his face in gold leaf and held a dead rabbit in his arms and talked to it about paintings that were hung in a gallery. This performance lasted for several hours and had elements of shamanistic ritual in the way he identified with the animal, but it was also a commentary on how we deify art, and overlook the immediacy of the lived moment. This approach to art may sound strange to some, yet Beuys is regarded as one of the most influential artists of the twentieth century.

One day Jonah came with the proposal to dig up a tree; he said this was the most appropriate metaphor for his own uprooting. He said he didn't want to understand this just on an intellectual level, but wanted the process to be embodied in the action of digging up the tree.

When he presented his proposal he was very clear about the process he and others would go through to make this happen and presented time lines and drawings in support of his proposal. He described these as an important first chapter of the ritual that allowed him to become more intimate with it. The initial part of the proposal was to choose a tree to uproot. Understandably this became an issue with some members of the community; but rather than make it an issue himself he gave very detailed reasons why he wanted to do this and why he chose a particular tree.

He explained that because of the impact of human populations in the San Jacinto Mountains, and the fire suppression that occurred as a result, the forest had become overpopulated with immature trees. In a pristine setting like the forests of Northern Baja, small fires burn all the time, creating a park-like environment that supports fewer, larger trees and a more diverse ecosystem. However, in the current manipulated environment where fires have been suppressed for over a hundred years, there is the constant danger of climax fires; with the trees so close together and competing for limited moisture the forest has become unhealthy. That is why forest management in these populated areas focuses on thinning.

This was all included in Jonah's presentation, and by the end of it and in other conversations the community was not only in support of his proposal but was enthusiastic about getting involved. This was Jonah's intent, because he felt that for the ritual to have real meaning it needed to have communal involvement.

The tree was a medium-sized incense cedar that stood in a grove of similar trees on a slope near the creek that runs through the property. This species was chosen because over the years it has supplanted other pine species that kept the ecosystem in balance. Like the students in the earlier example who spent time in contemplation to find a sense of place, Jonah spent time thinking about the environment before he started the process of uprooting. It reminded us of the respect and gratitude certain indigenous people show towards prey before and during the kill.

The uprooting took many days. His intention was to understand the anatomy of the tree through his own physical involvement in its uprooting. Uprooting therefore became self-revelation; the tap and root hairs were metaphors for his nervous system and his growing sensitivity. He invited others to help him and the site began to look like an archeological dig with students and faculty removing dirt and rocks from the root hairs, careful to preserve every facet of the root system.

After a period of a few weeks the tree was finally uprooted and ready to be transported to the school's gallery as part of a group senior show. This was one of the most beautiful and empowering parts of the ritual, because it required students and teachers alike to carry the tree half a mile up a hill, which was physically demanding, and reminiscent of other rituals that involve physical endurance.

The tree looked like some prehistoric animal exposed to the elements and cut off from its life support and presented a poignant metaphor for not only Jonah's specific condition but also for the alienation all of us feel at times. This was even more apparent in the stark environment of the gallery where the tree was truncated and inverted on a concrete and rebar support.

It was important to Jonah to have every part of the tree absorbed in to the ritual process, so on the night of the gallery opening he invited the community to a fire ceremony where the upper part and branches were burned and people were invited to write their own stories of displacement on paper and throw them into the fire. As well as being another way of including the wider community in the process, it expanded his own metaphorical language, enabling him to move past grieving into healing.

The connections between fire and hearth was apparent in the conversations that took place around the fire, and Jonah, as ritual instigator, was able to explicate the process further. This ritual illustrates the power of fire as a symbol of emergence and transformation, and in Jonah's case there is an oblique, but probably intentional, reference to the regenerative qualities of fire in the larger ecology, and how that became another metaphor for his own healing.

As part of the exhibit Jonathan drew a schematic of the process to describe how it had reverberated through the community. He drew the tree's cross-section with the roots radiating from the trunk and reaching into different parts of the community: the maintenance crew who helped with the planning, students and faculty who got involved in the uprooting, the carrying crew, all those displaced by Katrina, and the ecological communities that surrounded the tree.

He called this a "mandala" and emphasized that it wasn't finite or static but was constantly in flux. It became a map of emergence, and in a paradoxical way this gave new life to the tree. This series of pieces deepened his process of healing and pointed to the power of performance art based in ritual. It is also important to remember that this came about because Jonah was willing to embody this process fully and not assume that he could resolve it theoretically or conceptually.

For some, the description of this project may not conform with more conventional definitions of art. But Jonah's multilayered process represented the very best aspects of nontraditional and engaged art-making. Needless to say every major art school in the nation recruited him with scholarship offers. Jonah got a full scholarship to the Maryland Institute College of Art and graduated in 2010.

The story of Jonah brings the exploration of ritual full circle. It is a beautiful example of creativity, significance, and transformation. It is also a story that illustrates applied emergence: the open possibilities that self-organize into a structure of meaning and personal significance; the interaction of linear and nonlinear processes that create new layers of choice and experience; a willingness to embrace uncertainty and follow where it leads; a creative urgency that will not be denied and that is shared with a broader community; a playful state of mind that also challenges conventional thinking, but does so in a way that engendered trust; an example of fully embodied learning where conceptual understandings merge with authentic experience.

The attributes of openness, inquiry, and consolidation were present throughout the process, almost as an intuitive mindset. And a sense of ritual was integrated naturally and unconsciously as a mode of individual as well as communal participation. The distinction between time and space blurred as past and future arrived together in the present. Finally, we can see that Earth became the arbiter of experience reminiscent of Abram's observation that "only when space and time are reconciled into a single, unified field of phenomena does the encompassing earth become evident . . . as the very ground and horizon of all our knowing" (Abram, 1997, p. 217).

An inquiry into the narratives of emergent teaching reveals an iterative pattern of attributes and understandings that are not only consistent with scientific notions of emergence but are also evident in the authors' perceived experience. This recursive enfoldment creates an awareness for the teacher that can be both seen and felt while in the midst of the creative chaos so necessary for emergence and transformation.

These and other connections to the principle of emergence discussed in this book can be observed in Jonah's story. His narrative leads to a reconsideration of the very basis of education and our limited view of curriculum.

Chapter Eight

In the World

Teaching What Really Matters

Time is the substance of which I am made. Time is a river which sweeps me along, but I am the river; it is a fire which consumes me, but I am the fire.
—Jorge Luis Borges

As the quotation from Borges suggests, time and experience are intertwined. The commitments we choose—as individuals and a society—define who we are, shape our values, and create the will to act. So what is really important in the scheme of things? What is the purpose that will unfold in our life's journey? And what is the legacy of our "time?" The subject matter of curriculum is ultimately about the human experience, the world we live in, our place in that world, and the social systems we have created to sustain and organize our activity.

The world matters because we live in it. Meaning is biocentric; it is related to the life we are constantly creating. If what we teach does not connect students to the contingencies and questions of human experience then our teaching is stripped of meaning. Its only value becomes informational and instrumental, an economic commodity meant for general consumption. It loses the power to transform lives.

Emergence embeds the process of transformation with the iterated enfolding of information. What this means for curriculum is that when content is revisited from multiple perspectives, including subjectively important questions that arise from one's experience, it leads to a re-formation or transformation of not just the content but also the individual.

ıchers, also, are confronted with the deeper questions of purpose as
ѕ aspirations that bring or once brought joy and fulfillment to our work.
O'Donohue (1999) observes "You have come into rhythm with your longing.
Your work and action emerge naturally; you don't have to force yourself.
Your energy is immediate. Your passion is clear and creative" (in Nelson,
2011). As educators, we create an identity of "teacher" that can slowly separate us from our humanity—from those underlying inquiries that mark the
human journey. The journey we take reveals who we are.

Harste views curriculum as a process of inquiry, "a metaphor for the lives
we want to live and the people we want to be" (in Boran and Comber, 2001,
p. 1). Said another way, all curriculum needs to embed the questions *What
kind of world do I want to live in?* and *What kind of person do I want to be?*

When we make it possible for students to inquire into the issues and
questions of real significance to their lives and to the world they are part of, a
different kind of engagement takes place. Emergent teaching becomes a partnership of inquiry and discovery, an ongoing conversation of significance,
transformation, and service.

This chapter is inspired by ten metaphorical woodcuts by Kakuan Shien
of twelfth-century China, based on traditional images that are older still. The
images tell a story of self-discovery, personal transformation, and engaged
service in the world. Ironically, what was discovered was there all along.
Such is the paradox of transformation—everything is different although
nothing has changed.

TEN OX-HERDING IMAGES

The story portrayed by these woodcuts begins with a young boy searching
for an ox that has gone missing. The ox is actually visible but the boy is
looking in the wrong direction. This first image is sometimes referred to as
"the search." It is a story of a divided self in search for wholeness, the
integration of one's inner and outer worlds. At the beginning of any search
one is motivated yet burdened by questions. There is confusion and disquiet.
One does not search unless there is a personal connection to the question.

Emergent teaching seeks to focus on authentic questions and curiosities
that have the potential to fully engage the student. The process of discovery
may begin with the teacher but must be owned by the student.

The second image is entitled "finding the tracks." This image shows the
boy running now and gleeful because he has discerned the path. His head is
lifted toward the clouds in the sky. Confusion gives way to discernment
when patterns can be observed. There is a sense that if one stays with the
inquiry, more will be discovered. The journey is not over, but persistence
will lead to more understanding.

The act of following is significant for both the student and the teacher. The student follows the inquiry; the teacher follows the student. This insight is consistent with neuroscience research that emphasizes the importance of patterning in the construction of meaning. The recognition of patterns is crucial for understanding (Caine et al., 1999). Every teacher lives for those "a-ha" moments when students start to "get it." When this happens external motivation is largely unnecessary, the student "wants" to learn. A teacher cannot force "a-ha" moments.

In emergent teaching, teachers help students make sense of their observations throughout the inquiry; they guide, not direct, the process. "Finding the tracks" is significant for any process of transformation and self-inquiry.

"Glimpsing the ox" is the title of the third woodcut. Here, the boy looks over his shoulder and sees the ox. There is a hint of surprise here as if the ox is not where the boy expected. Serendipity is often an integral part of self-discovery. One begins by searching in an organized and systematic way; but as new information is enfolded and processed, this often gives way to surprises and intuitions that could not have been planned.

This is especially true in emergent teaching. The idea of self-reference in quantum mechanics, for example, implies that what one discovers about the outer world cannot be separated from the inner world of the inquirer. The boy in these images is glimpsing the integrated nature of his inner and outer worlds, but does not fully understand what this means.

The fourth image shows that the boy has lassoed the ox, but the ox is pulling him wherever it wants to go. Here the boy is now integrating his inner and outer worlds but does not have the skills or the discipline he needs. Once one's perceptions of our inner and outer worlds begin to change, there is uncertainty about what this means and where it might lead.

As we saw in the chapter on creativity, a degree of chaos is needed for new order to emerge. Remember, however, that from the perspective of emergence, chaos is not unmanageable; it is simply open and free to self-organize. Students need help with this. They can begin to see multiple possibilities in their inquiry but may lack the skills or tools to look more deeply. The inquiry is not done. In emergent teaching, this is where skill development, methodologies for deeper inquiry, and creative implications start to occur naturally.

The next image, "taming the ox," shows the boy casually leading the ox by the rope. There is an implied sense of direction and the suggestion that a degree of discipline has made it possible to harness the potential of a more integrated self.

In emergent teaching, the teacher observes when a student's synthesis of understanding has more direction. Helping the student develop new skills allows her to pursue something meaningful and original. Guidance is still necessary but it is gentle and nourishing. It is meant to encourage further integration still. The image of taming the ox indicates that old assumptions and misperceptions still hang on. This is often true of students as well.

The sixth image is of the boy riding the ox effortlessly while playing a flute. The ox, untethered, nevertheless seems to know the way. This image is called "riding the ox home." The boy and the ox are in perfect harmony.

Applying this to emergent teaching, when students are able to integrate learning into their lives, the joy of self-discovery is its own reward. The addition of the flute in this woodcut is interesting. It suggests that what is assimilated deeply will find new expression. Borges (1967) writes "To see in the day or in the year a symbol / Of mankind's day and of his years, / To transform the outrage of the years / Into a music, a rumor, and a symbol, / To see in death a sleep, and in the sunset / A sad gold, of such is Poetry" (p. 89). The urge to express the joy of meaningful, integrated learning is a natural tendency that does not need coercion, just opportunity.

In the seventh image, the boy sits alone outside a thatched hut contemplating the moon. There is a peaceful feeling that emanates from this image. It is called "ox forgotten" and portrays a moment when the divided self, the struggle between one's inner and outer world, is now illuminated by the bright serenity and clarity of the full moon. Now, there is no need to look for the ox; it is where it needs to be. And there is no sense of division, only silence, contemplation, awareness.

This image is particularly interesting from the point of view of emergent teaching. It would seem that the sixth image would make the story complete, but this seventh image helps us see the power and importance of contemplation, of quiet reflection, the "soaking in" of mystery and understanding. Such wisdom is analytical and intuitive, imageless yet full of content.

We don't engage in this type of consolidation very much in schools or even recognize its value. Yet more and more there is evidence that slowing down the mental processes of thought allows a different kind of wisdom to emerge.

Claxton (1997) writes that with the rise of the new sciences of chaos and complexity must come a reevaluation of the slower ways of knowing; of intuition as an essential complement to reason. One who has cultivated this way of knowing is described as being able to attend to the nuances and connective patterns that arise from complex questions. He describes it this way:

> She is able to 'let things speak', to see what is actually there, and not, as Hesse put it, to observe everything in 'a cloudy mirror of your own desire'. She is able to make good use of clues and hints. She is able to analyse and scrutinize,

> but also to daydream and ruminate. She is able to ask questions and collaborate, but is also able to keep silent and contemplate. She is able to be both literal and metaphorical, articulate and visionary, scientific and poetic. (p. 220)

In a similar way, learning that is transformative lets one see more clearly the reality of oneself and the world. Reflection and contemplation are keys to an emergent learning that is transformative.

The eighth image is an empty circle entitled "both ox and self forgotten." When there is a letting go of what something has to be or what it has to mean, there is a kind of empty space that can be felt and perceived. There is an acceptance that does not need to be filled with some new category. Of course this sounds very Eastern, and it is. But this opening of a space where wisdom can emerge on its own is something that is part of Western traditions as well as indigenous cultures.

The ancient Chinese ideogram for wisdom implied "sweeping away the clutter." In this space the heart/mind does its own work. In classes and workshops we have created circles of listening where insights and understandings can be shared, not imposed. In these circles, connections are made to real-life concerns in relation to new insights and realizations. It is a powerful space, both individually and socially. It leads to consolidations that simply could not have been predicted. It is often the case that previous concepts and categories are either dropped as unnecessary or reconceived.

When one of us asks, "What are the obstructions to you teaching the way your heart desires to teach?" many items listed are mental obstructions, fears, projected expectations of others rather than real barriers. There is a realization of how our mental assumptions and models create much of our experience and how we perpetuate these ideas as if they were tangible truths. For the authors, the image of an empty circle in "ox and self forgotten" suggests a continuous process.

The ninth image depicts a flowering tree, a hummingbird, and flowers falling into a flowing river. It is called "returning to the source." The simplicity of nature and its natural processes are shown here to be complete and perfect just as they are. Nothing needs to be added or taken away.

This is an important realization, and it allows one to approach the world with a state of confidence and purpose. Once learners realize there is no division between themselves and their knowing, they are free to act purposefully in the world. In other words, knowing becomes integrated into who one is. Ontological knowing calls for action. It is not a passive relationship to information; rather this kind of knowing propels the learner into making a difference in the world.

Education becomes an emergent response in which learning naturally extends to an active engagement of self-creation in the world. This is a bit different from an ideological sense of praxis in that it is the natural unfolding of a personal response to what we know and who we are. This sense of "returning to the source" is in fact a grappling with the question "What do I do with this knowledge?" It represents a situated cognitive response that implies meaning, significance, and action.

This leads to the final and tenth woodcut, "in the world," sometimes called "in the marketplace." Here the young boy who started out on the journey of self-discovery according to traditional interpretations has achieved realization and become a sage. He goes to the marketplace where he is now able to help others and be of service. It is significant that in the story represented by these ten woodcuttings, the end of learning leads to service.

These ten woodcuttings themselves represent a circle. They symbolize our natural state and how, if engaged in the journey, our natural qualities and wisdom become activated and sensitized. This is consistent with recent understandings of the development of the cerebral cortex that show the role of empathy, altruism, and caring in cognitive function. It also relates to the "heart-based" considerations of learning in which loving-kindness and compassion are valued as important and legitimate educational outcomes. There are also echoes of critical theory where conscientization brings learners into a responsive relationship with the world.

Emergent teaching provides an opportunity for students to consider how others can benefit from what they have learned through their inquiry. By confronting the provocative questions of *What kind of world do I want to live in?* and *What kind of person do I want to be?* emergent teaching can open students to consider more deeply the questions related to "what really matters."

Transformation is both personal and social in that one's knowing is situated *in the world*. The image of "in the world" or "in the marketplace" provides a sense of relationship between self-discovery and service. The marketplace is everyday life, anything and everything. The ordinariness that the boy in the ox-herd series returned to was his original state but with a new awareness of what this means. By accepting that we are constantly emerging, and in emergence there is no final destination or conclusion, we open ourselves to all possibilities. This acceptance is a recognition of our innate wisdom.

A JOURNEY, NOT AN END

One of the insights we can take from the ox-herd series is that transformation is a continuous journey rather than a destination. Something emerges from the journey itself that is situated inside one's experience. It is as though some aspect of oneself has been found that was always there but now cries out for acceptance and for natural expression not dependent on a sense of personal need.

This sense of life as a journey has provoked questions of value for millennia. Hadot (2005) outlines how questions of ultimate significance have guided practical activity since the early Greeks. Within the framework of a deliberate worldview, Hadot shows how each of the Greek schools of thought contemplated death on a daily basis. It was one of the most important aspects of personal cultivation and positive influence in daily life.

He argues that for the Greeks, philosophy was intended as a conversion of one's attention from the external world to one's interior experience where purposes, questions, commitments, and aspirations are born. Contemplating death leads to contemplating life—to one's ongoing birth and development and to those things that matter most in one's life.

Randy Pausch's *The Last Lecture* (2008) is a poignant example of this kind of dual focus. Pausch was a popular science professor who developed pancreatic cancer. Knowing that he was dying, he wanted his "last lecture" to be directed to the hearts and minds of his students, not in a maudlin or sympathetic way, but in order to encourage them to embrace life and living. His book explains the importance of child-like dreaming and the willingness to create a life of adventure through dedicating oneself to hard work and following your dreams.

He emphasized the immense satisfaction of helping others reach their dreams and living a life of service. And with great passion he gave examples in his own life in which kindness, love, integrity, and generosity were central to living a meaningful and happy life. It is in the journey of life that significance and meaning finds its multiple destinations and becomes a transformative agent for all of us. Sam explains how this has worked in his own life:

> During the writing of this chapter I learned that my father was in the last stages of lung cancer. The idea of "what really matters" came home to me in the context of real experience. The process of dying, the significance of relationship, and ultimately the quality and meaning of life came into focus in a way that was tangible and closely personal. Ironically, when faced with imminent loss and the certainty of dying, the mind turns not so much to death but to life.
>
> The legacy of values and the multiple acts of love from my father were what my mind turned to. My desire to make him comfortable and receive each day as a gift became clearly evident. And the conversations lost the banality of the unimportant. In their place were remembering, acceptance, appreciation, letting go, and the immediate focus on the next necessity that presented itself. The trappings of what we commonly take as important fell away on their own, and in their place was a renewed questioning of deep values, personal commitments, and life intentions.
>
> Upon my father's death, I became absorbed once again with the mundane necessities of funeral arrangements and other details. But now away from those distractions, I contemplate almost daily how to live a life of greater significance and service. Somehow the legacy of death turns itself inside out to emphasize questions about what is most important in life. Both grief and

gratitude enfold themselves into this ongoing, open question. And as I consider the certainty of my own death, the question weighs heavily upon me, not as a burden but as opportunity. I can see myself in the story of the woodcuts as I constantly renew my own journey of self-discovery.

As represented in the woodcuts, life as a journey contains at all stages the seeds of transformation. And yet the very nature of transformation is a discovery of what is already there. Lanza (2009) refers to the "unfolding of life" as an embedded awareness that occurs within one's mind when internal and external perceptions are no longer distinguishable from one's identity (p. 39). Perhaps it is awareness itself that is really at the heart of any transformation.

Instructionally, when teachers give students the opportunity to search their own experience over time, looking for patterns, shifts, and new understandings learning takes on a different kind of significance. There is a relationship among the questions, investigations, findings, and responses that have integrated meaning.

This sense of wondering, of making significance, can be seen in a portion of poem from a student in Sam's class as she participates inside her own personal and intellectual journey.

> I start in hexagon form
> Curse you! You many sided structure
> A platform for a journey I'm not sure I want to
> Go on
> Infinite planes, lines
> Hiding in walls, floors, boards, desks
> Here starts the neurobiology of stress
> Discerning openness
> Interest forthcoming,
> breathe, move, greet
> self, other, earth, sky
> Good Morning, Good Morning, Good Morning!
> The flow of energy and information
> Inseparable: informative meaning
> Created within, wired to connect
> Education separated: meaningless information
> Flat
> I move off this six sided hex and am gone
> Meandering perception
> Of situation, environment
> Static classroom, post-office lighting, no windows
> Adding to, creating, changing, altering my
> Experience in the space, out of the space
> Whole organism learning, am I open to it
> Or just another closed system
> No
> I am open to

Joy
Belief in experiential
Education
In using my body
To learn its experience
It's what I've always preferred
But tried to fit
round hole square peg
you know the story
I wonder at the others now
What do they think of all this
Who are these bodies of life before me
the present professor
the unformed group
What needs my attention
as a student, a teacher, a partner, a daughter, a friend
What doesn't need my attention
So many things~I know them all
too well

There is a felt sense of journey in this poem. One can feel the movement of mind, of struggle, of questioning, and the consolidation of meaning that is taking place. It illustrates how content and life are interconnected for this student—how the external and internal are integral parts of the same process. The student is not separated from her knowing, but instead uses it to explore her own concerns.

When the curriculum is merely a stationary destination to be reached, there is an inherent separation from real life and an implied imposition of legitimized knowledge. Such hegemony often creates a distance between the student and their experience, whether it is personal or cultural.

Teaching what matters is a journey in which one becomes connected not only to the content but to the processes of inquiry and, in so doing, experiences an integration of understandings that can (and must) be expressed in the world. Just as the processes of self-discovery illustrated by the ox-herd series reach full circle "in the world," so must the journey and the destination of learning. Teaching that emphasizes the journey, the processes, the integration of meaning is not devoid of a destination; rather the end results usually are more personalized and serve as springboards for action or for deeper exploration.

Miller (2001) describes the aim for personal integration and social awareness as transformative learning. He presents a balanced approach of transmission, transaction, and transformation as a holistic vision of education. For Miller, teaching strategies that facilitate the transformative aims of integration and awareness are more invitational in nature. They are cooperative and creative in their processes. There is an emphasis on journal writing, storytelling, dramatic play, and service-oriented options. Assessment is more qualitative, formative, and presentational. There is a sense of engagement and ownership in what was learned or experienced because knowing becomes related to the life of the student and the learning community.

The view of teaching as a transformative journey is also explored by O'Sullivan (1999) who describes transformation as the structural shifts of basic premises as well as shifts of consciousness that alter one's sense of being. He builds his argument from the work of ecologist Thomas Berry and places society within a mega-framework of ecological history. A society's identity is in part tied to its relationship with nature.

O'Sullivan promotes the need to understand personal and social issues from this larger perspective. His hope is tied to the creation of new visions for alternative approaches to living in which social justice, peace, and personal fulfillment are intertwined. He clearly represents transformation as an ongoing journey with a diversity of destinations—all emergent and transitional in the flow of time.

TRANSFORMATION AS INTEGRATION

Once educators are committed to teaching what really matters, content becomes a vehicle for deeper significance and a natural marker for responsive engagement in the world. There is a greater emphasis on alternative ways of knowing, cross-disciplinary approaches to inquiry, and creative application of concepts, ideas, and information. For example, systems thinking becomes especially relevant in the life sciences as well as in history, sociology, and political economy. No matter what the content, opportunities abound to understand and explore what the information means in terms of the dynamically interacting processes relevant to what is being studied.

In addition to understanding the world in terms of interactive systems, Clark (1996) encourages the use of essential questions to take ordinary content to more substantive levels of inquiry. The teacher frames questions around not just what is important to know but, more significantly, what is essential to understand and explore in more depth.

Clark creates four broad contexts that for him define our time: the subjective context, the context of time, the symbolic context, and the ecosystem context. Focus questions such as "What does it mean to be human?" or "How does one live responsibly in a global community?" are explored through a matrix of new questions that integrate various contextual perspectives with various disciplines.

Below is an example of this process by using a theme that explores how one lives responsibly in a global village:

- The subjective context with natural sciences: "How am I part of any system?
- The context of time and natural science: "How do systems change?"
- The symbolic context and natural science: "How do systems work?"
- The ecological context and natural science: "What is the impact of natural systems on cultural systems?"

Essential questions are not merely intellectual exercises; they relate to the real world and to the lives of students. Emergent teaching builds upon this kind of questioning and provides opportunities and options that invite students to engage in real discovery and integration. These ideas reflect the allegory of the ox-herd series in that the boy's transformation was in realizing that he was naturally integrated *in the world.*

Emergent teaching is *naturally* differentiated. By its nature it is outside the box and encourages the natural curiosity and interests of students. It can be individual or group-oriented, subject-specific or more thematic. It can be inside or outside the curriculum, thus adaptable to many different contexts and situations.

Perceiving learning as a journey that incorporates the subjective experience and creativity of the student is a necessary attitude that makes emergent teaching possible. Just as the boy in the allegory engages in his own journey, ultimately our students must do the same.

TEACHING WHAT REALLY MATTERS REQUIRES UNLEARNING

When space is provided for meaning to be integrated into one's life and applied in the world, many shifts can occur in a student's previous assumptions and beliefs. In our experience, such shifts or transformations are necessary for new constructions of meaning to take root. Then those new constructions nurture alternative understandings and actions in the world.

At a neurological level this process happens throughout a person's development, but especially at particular physiological "windows." The altered, or *plasticized*, neural pathways allow sometimes huge developmental leaps to occur. Unlearning occurs throughout our lives and is a necessary aspect of transformation.

Unlearning is crucial because our brains map and process information in somewhat predictable patterns. These patterns self-reinforce, so that a person's perceptual world becomes self-sustaining, supported by previous beliefs, assumptions, and conditioning. Hypnotist Steve Taubman (2005), in talking about hypnotism, explains that we are all hypnotized. He sees his job as first un-hypnotizing his clients, loosening certain perceptual beliefs so that a space is created to affirm other perceptions and the possibilities they may offer. Instead of being limited by a faux reality that is accepted as given, we can replace them with beliefs and perceptions that liberate and free us to develop new patterns of possibility. This is very consistent with what we know of neuroplasticity.

Not only does this apply to the conditioning of our own lives, but students come to the classroom every day with habitually conditioned beliefs that often limit the unleashing of their own creative potential. How do we help ourselves and others unlearn these limiting beliefs?

While the research is quite new in this area, Walter Freeman's work is quite revealing. Freeman showed how oxytocin functions as both a neuro-peptide and a neuromodulator. Oxytocin has been popularly described as the "love hormone" because of its association with love-making and with the early phases of parenting. It is different from dopamine excitement in that it is accompanied by feelings of tenderness, warmth, bonding, and connection.

What is really interesting is that oxytocin helps dislodge and unlearn neural circuits shaped by feelings of separation and isolation and replaces them with relational dispositions like caring and selflessness. Neuromodulators are much more powerful than neurotransmitters. They dull the patterns of habitual information processing and allow for new patterns to be established.

A selfless concern for the welfare of others is not just an ideal that appears in wisdom traditions throughout history; it represents a powerful process of neural change and transformation. Love may be much more of a practical key to changing the world—and ourselves—than we have been willing to recognize.

So, what is it that needs to be unlearned? This is a recurrent question and requires multiple contexts and subjective responses. Unlearning asks us to be aware of that which is no longer productive and be willing to be open to new understandings and possibilities. Unlearning has implications for building human capacity but it also has implications for our culture as well. Each one of us, and our society as a whole, has the capacity to unlearn old ways of being while creating a new set of creative possibilities. A purposeful, responsive education embraces this kind of transformative thinking and lets it emerge throughout the curriculum.

A central question for any kind of transformative education, whatever the context, is *What does this require me to unlearn?* This is the heart of emergent teaching. Unlearning and learning are entangled with each other in that the emergence of new patterns and dispositions requires the casting off of previously dominant patterns of thinking and action. The boy in the ox-herd series was transformed, not because he changed but because a new pattern of being was integrated and subsequent patterns of action emerged.

PRIORITIES, VALUES, AND ACTION

What guides an educator when faced with the question of teaching what really matters? Already we have suggested that emergent teaching taps into the heart of our humanity, to the personal journeys and questions that engage our students, and to the processes of transformation where unproductive perceptions and assumptions are unlearned and new visions of possibility are put into place.

Certainly, each of us has our own commitments that we feel compelled to champion or emphasize. As educators though, our task is not to impose yet another way of thinking onto our students but instead to open them to the arena of important ideas and dispositions so their own inquiries, creative energy, and responsive action can unfold.

Pink (2006), for example, argues that citizens in the twenty-first century will need to develop and use what he calls "six high-concept, high-touch senses" that for him are more representative of the mind's natural wholeness. He counterbalances function with *design*, argument with *story*, focus with *symphony*, seriousness with *play*, and accumulation with *meaning* (pp. 65–67). For Pink, these senses will increasingly define the challenges of the future.

The role of education has often been tied to our visions of the needs of the future. Whether it be in the area of skills or dispositions, focusing on the future is one way to consider what is important, what are imminent challenges, and what direction we as a society want to commit to.

Usually, however, these discussions are on the periphery of education or they are tied to political ideologies that do little to promote genuine dialogical reflection and interchange. While the topic of change is often discussed, the structural components of the educational system receive most of the attention, often without the sociological understanding of the relationship between structural and functional stasis and adaptive, innovative change.

In some instances there is an attempt to bridge the need for structural stability and the concurrent need to shift the way we think and engage new processes of learning in that endeavor. Where Pink refers to "senses" Gardner (2007) discusses what he calls "minds" that our society needs to cultivate. These "minds" have traditional, even classical elements, but Gardner frames them with a contemporary voice.

He begins with the Disciplined Mind where he champions the value of disciplinary thinking. But he ties this kind of thinking to specifically human activity and social progress. He reminds us that the heart and essence of our disciplines is found in the processes and methodologies of thinking, not just in the accumulation of content. And since the disciplines as frames or containers are insufficient in and of themselves, educators need to see beyond their limited and fragmentary nature.

So Gardner moves on to discuss the Synthesizing Mind. Pulling together information and understandings that are relevant to particular issues and important questions requires not just new kinds of skills but opportunities to readjust our thinking. This means finding a balance between what is too narrow and what is too broad. It means having a willingness to play in the arena of context.

Gardner's next emphasis is the Creative Mind. He bases his interpretation of this "mind" on ideas of craft, mastery, and originality. He does not locate creativity only in the arts but rather relates it to cognitive processes that are part of each and every discipline. For Gardner, removing obstacles to creativity is much more effective in building capacity than a particular method or strategy. For example, racing after the one correct answer or the singular method of perceiving a solution is counter to any effort to increase the abilities to create and innovate.

His next emphasis is the Respectful Mind. Here, Gardner emphasizes the value of diversity and the need to engage with others who have different cultural perspectives, have different life agendas, but also share real and common human concerns.

His final designation is the Ethical Mind. For Gardner, this means an emphasis on our responsibilities in the larger scheme of things. We each have a sphere of influence that more or less defines our context. Within that sphere, how can our actions respond to particular needs and how can those have a larger influence still? Our lives are made up of a variety of roles, and each of those roles entails its own expectations. So the ethical mind calls us to be accountable for our actions in each and every context—as a student, a worker, a parent, a child, a citizen, a friend.

For Gardner these "five minds" represent opportunities to make education more relevant to students while at the same time helping to create necessary skills, understandings, and dispositions that are needed in the world. They represent a more complete vision for education in our society.

Pink and Gardner are not presented here in order to advocate for their particular positions, but to show examples of what it means to raise the question "what really matters?" In the allegory of the ox-herd series we can see that each of us has the seed of our own answer to this question, not in some finalized sense, but rather an answer that relates to our own journey or inquiry.

When educators engage in this journey together, the insights and opportunities to support substantive and significant change are expanded and increased. Such is the story of one attempt to articulate what is really important in a global sense when diverse nations and cultures came together to consider humanity's precarious position in the twenty-first century. It is the story of the International Earth Charter.

THE INTERNATIONAL EARTH CHARTER: AN EXAMPLE

The origins of the story of the International Earth Charter began in 1987 when interest was expressed in creating a universal declaration that could guide the thinking of nations, local governments, corporations, civil society groups, and individuals. In 1990, prior to the first World Summit on the environment held in Rio de Janeiro, a focused effort was initiated to see if a declaration that represented the views and interests of diverse regions of the world could actually become a reality.

Imagine the difficulty of creating a positive vision of the future that would be acceptable and practical to a diversity of nations, cultures, religions, ethnicities, genders, political ideologies, corporate interests, and individuals throughout the world. Imagine a deliberate attempt to not just invite the participation of politicians but of local interests from around the world, indigenous groups as well as leaders of major religious traditions, voices that are often forgotten or marginalized.

Over a period of ten years, this process led to International Earth Charter, perhaps the most participative and inclusive document ever produced. It is a product of a decade-long, worldwide, cross-cultural dialogue and represents common goals and shared values expressed and refined by the peoples of the world as they considered a sustainable and workable vision of the future for all humankind.

This vision is expressed in terms of principles meant to orient our thinking when considering practical action that affects one's immediate interests and the interests of all. It was presented to UNESCO in March of 2000 and ratified as a global statement of principles to guide the inhabitants of Earth toward a sustainable and peaceful future. It later became the ethical foundation for the United Nations' Decade for Education for Sustainable Development. The Earth Charter is a nongovernmental organization dedicated to promoting sustainable ways of living based on a set of common ethical values. Below, Sam relates his own story of participating in the Earth Charter and how this has led to new considerations of "teaching what really matters."

> My story with the International Earth Charter began years ago when I traveled to the United Nations' University for Peace located in Ciudad Colon, Costa Rica. I was interested in studying a program in Peace Education. What I discovered was a program based on the principles of the Earth Charter. The program's founder, Dr. Abelardo Brenes, introduced me to the charter and I was immediately taken with the extensive and inclusive process that led to a sense of shared vision. The heart of the vision for me was the articulation of four broad commitments:

Earth and life in all its diversity.

ıgnize that all beings are interdependent and every form of life
regardless of its worth to human beings.

n faith in the inherent dignity of all human beings and in the
...tellectual, artistic, ethical, and spiritual potential of humanity.

2. **Care for the community of life with understanding, compassion, and
   love.**

   a. Accept that with the right to own, manage, and use natural resources
   comes the duty to prevent environmental harm and to protect the rights of
   people.

   b. Affirm that with increased freedom, knowledge, and power comes
   increased responsibility to promote the common good.

3. **Build democratic societies that are just, participatory, sustainable,
   and peaceful.**

   a. Ensure that communities at all levels guarantee human rights and
   fundamental freedoms and provide everyone an opportunity to realize his
   or her full potential.

   b. Promote social and economic justice, enabling all to achieve a secure
   and meaningful livelihood that is ecologically responsible.

4. **Secure Earth's bounty and beauty for present and future generations.**

   a. Recognize that the freedom of action of each generation is qualified
   by the needs of future generations.

   b. Transmit to future generations values, traditions, and institutions that
   support the long-term flourishing of Earth's human and ecological communities.

I think what impressed me so much was how holistically conceived these
commitments are and how they lead to natural discussions and conversations
of what they mean in the practical world. They came across to me as going
beyond ideology, as statements that reflect the true character of human concerns, and they expressed the interconnected nature of what it might mean to
live sustainably.

Over the years as I have shared the Earth Charter with my students and
colleagues, I have encountered a wide range of responses. Some students are
carried away with inspired enthusiasm. They have encountered the limitations
of critical theory where they have been awakened to the importance of social
justice and equality but have been demoralized by the hegemony of our institutions and the lack of a positive vision. They see the Earth Charter as a natural
theoretical extension.

Yet for many students and teachers, these principles and commitments still
remain largely theoretical. A rather common initial reaction is more cynical—
the statements are not practical given the severe realities and conditions of our
time; they are "merely" ideals that sound good but have little prospect for
reality. A third reaction is the perception that the Earth Charter is presented as
belief statements that surreptitiously promote a singular philosophical, political, and religious orthodoxy.

At first these mixed reactions were discouraging. But then I realized that
statements alone can seem like calcified content just like any other curricular
emphasis. Presenting the Earth Charter as something to merely believe in or

endorse stripped it of its potency. Its real power lies in the conversation, the inquiry of what is important. The four broad commitments are opportunities to consider who we are, what our purpose is, what we value, and how we act in the context of real life.

As an applied philosopher, I realized that ethical conversations could be created around the Earth Charter that could bring the field of ethics to life.

—In terms of traditional *virtue* ethics, the Earth Charter principles open up conversations that deal with one's character and beliefs.

—As a discussion of *situational* ethical questions, the inquiry centers on more instrumental concerns, of the tension between self-interest and the common good.

—A more *rationally oriented* approach to ethics invites the exploration of assumptions and the philosophical consistency between beliefs and actions, as well as technical analysis of words and meanings.

—Finally, a more *existential* discussion moves into the subjectivity of one's choices and decisions. How are these reconciled with the inherent contradictions of choice-making, with socially obligatory expectations, with institutional realities, etc.?

However, even more important than these philosophically oriented discussions on ethics, I realized that the Earth Charter provided a vehicle to contextualize compelling ideas within a situated, real-life environment where its meanings and significance could be explored *in action*. Here the idea was to imagine what a principle might look like when embedded within a specific context like a classroom, a school, a family, an organization, or a community. This kind of inquiry, over time, leads to natural action from within and a natural laboratory to learn, create, question, and serve.

When the Earth Charter is used as a basis for conversation and when its principles are placed in the context of real life and real situations, it finds voice and ownership in the lives and actions of students. Many of my graduate students who teach in public schools have used the Earth Charter in their own classrooms.

One teacher created conversations on classroom conduct based on discussions of respect, dignity, compassion, responsibility, and freedom. Even first graders responded to these ideas. Besides being integrated into the class rules, a concrete understanding was rediscovered and iterated through children's literature, everyday experience, and events they encountered daily. Several of my students created gardens and special community projects, not because they built it into their lesson plans but because the projects arose naturally through focused conversation and concern.

Of course, the Earth Charter principles find a natural integration into established curricula in the social studies and sciences, but I believe they are much more powerful when integrated into a classroom or school culture. One former student of mine created an outline for an after-school program focused on "Doing Good." Other students focused on life lessons, values, and respect. Still others created conversations and activities built around inquiry of such concepts as diversity, peace, nonviolent communication, leadership, and global citizenship.

A wonderful program called Roots and Shoots developed by conservationist and primatologist Jane Goodall is a strong endorser of Earth Charter principles. Roots and Shoots creates student-led projects based on knowledge, compassion, and action.

In one Roots and Shoots program I visited in Costa Rica, high school students decided to study ways to protect endangered turtle species. This led to a field trip to work with scientists and participate in various ecological projects. In the process, they turned their attention to the communities surrounding these habitats and realized that the local people were one key to protecting the turtles. The students developed a sociological survey to gain more knowledge of the community's views of the turtles and their needs. The survey indicated a need for ecological education, economic development, and medical assistance.

Over time these high school students created educational materials for the community, raised money to build a small local clinic, and petitioned several doctors to visit the community on a rotating basis to provide services to the community. In talking to the students, it was clear that each one's life had been changed by these acts of loving-kindness and service.

Teaching what is important does not have to compete with academic requirements. On the contrary, in this case the study of science, ecology, sociology, and politics was enhanced by a service-oriented initiative of being "in the world." Teachers throughout the world engage their students in community projects that reflect an ongoing conversation in which the values and ideals of the Earth Charter are brought to life, not in a narrowly defined, prescriptive way, but in a way that engages the creativity and natural concern of students.

As an example of teaching what really matters, my experience with the Earth Charter taught me once again that real learning emerges from experience, inquiry, and awareness. It is an embodied process realized in action and in community. While the consolidation and significance is always uniquely individual, a shared culture is created that is tolerant and understanding, reflecting both our commonalities and our differences.

Ultimately, "what really matters" must be acted upon "in the world," within a cultural and social context that has meaning. Otherwise the real potency of ideas never becomes enlivened. I have come to see my own role as a teacher as bringing ideas to life in the context of real experience.

IN THE WORLD—IN THE MARKETPLACE

The tenth woodcut of the ox-herd series suggests that the process of self-discovery does not end with oneself but in the understanding that there is no real distinction between self and others. Being in the world is an act of compassion and authentic service that emerges from one's natural engagement. It is not contrived or forced.

Bernie Glassman Roshi (2003), who founded the Zen Peacemaker Order, exemplifies this point: "I chose not to live in a monastery. I got involved in business, social action, and peacemaking. So for me the question became 'what are the forms in business, social action, and peacemaking that can help us see the oneness of society, the interdependence of life . . . that will move each of us towards the realization and actualization of the enlightened way, which is none other than peacemaking?" (p. 11).

One could say that true service emerges out of who one is. Teaching what really matters is a larger consideration of one's personal journey, and providing a format, a vision, an authentic purpose for students to act in the world, may be the most important part of learning.

Discovering these visions and purposes involves the recognition that one's inner life matters. Helping students develop the skill and capacity to be more aware of their thoughts, feelings, and stresses—their inner world—has led to some amazing results. Not only do students become more emotionally resilient, goal oriented, and academically successful, they also act toward others with more kindness and selfless concern.

Programs like HeartMath, Mindfulness, CARE (Cultivating Awareness and Resilience in Education), MindUp, Passageways, and the Courage to Teach have demonstrated significantly positive impacts on academic achievement. But more importantly for our discussion, such programs help students deal constructively with emotional distress, develop more positive attitudes toward others, and see their world in more optimistic terms.

These programs tend to offer children and teenagers more self-awareness and agency. They do not feel powerless to affect their world. Such programs also have tremendous impact on teachers. Transformation is life-changing because, just as in the story in the ox-herd series, through transformation we discover our own truths and find that heart-based decisions outweigh more egocentric concerns.

Thus, we come full circle. The story of the ox-herd series begins with both inquiry and journey. It continues with the boy's willingness to explore both his outer world and inner world, eventually integrating them as he rides into the marketplace. His story doesn't stop with discovery, but continues through the consolidation of personal truths and an awareness of deep insights into his nature. This is a nonseparated identity that blurs the distinction between self and others while also living forth one's truth *in the world.*

Chapter Nine

When the Curriculum Disappears

A Holistic Perspective

Throughout this book we have tried to explore through a modified methodology of narrative inquiry some of the critical elements of what might be called *emergent teaching*. Rather than provide a strict definition or create an explanatory theory, and then demonstrate that theory with practical examples and strategies, a more indirect and nonlinear approach has been used.

Through personal stories, myths, and analogies the idea of emergence has been examined both from its scientific foundation within chaos and complexity theory and from a metaphorical perspective of multithreaded tales. Although the dominant vantage point has been from our own experiences, insights into the concept of emergence as an authentic reality rather than primarily a mathematically based phenomenon of complexity science has been the goal.

It is the "space" of emergence that has been explored—that indeterminate mixture of chaos and boundary where something determinate emerges. This notion of emergence resides in one's subjective experience and is laden with meaning. When processed, shared, and honored it has the potential to transform.

Throughout this book there has been the implicit assumption that emergent teaching primarily operates at the edges of the curriculum, at its borders. This does not mean that it could not play a more central role in education or that the elements discussed cannot be applied to instructional practices at all levels. However, in the present-day climate of outcome standards, arbitrarily paced content expectations, and one-size-fits-all approaches to instruction, the idea of emergent teaching runs counter to the general mindset prevalent in most educational institutions.

And yet teachers and students yearn for more authentic opportunities for significant learning—learning that relates to real life, important questions, and transformative possibilities. Many, perhaps most, instructional practices designed to promote the mass consumption of standardized information have departed from any real foundation of learning theory, especially research in the neurosciences and cognitive sciences that understand learning from the perspective of meaning, personal significance, applied action, decision-making, and integrated social-emotional development.

The attributes present in emergent teaching provide a new lens through which *any* instructional model can be viewed. The qualities of teaching from the heart remain relevant to *any* educational context. Genuine concern for students and relating education to their subjective experience, their dreams, their cultures, and their questions remain an aspiration for *any* teacher. Creative engagement, contemplation, and the more extensive use of physical modalities that embody and consolidate content are fundamental to *any* learning process. And extending oneself and one's knowing into the world with compassionate concern for others is an outcome worthy of *any* curriculum.

Each of these elements is a critical indicator of an educational environment conducive to the cultivation of human capacity. So how can educators view curriculum in a way that invites these attributes to find a natural place?

CURRICULUM AS CONVERSATION

The history of curriculum is usually presented as the prescribed outcomes that have been considered valuable in a given society. This assumes that formal education is an enterprise meant to socialize students into the norms, values, and ideologies of a nation-state, religious worldview, or imposed political or colonial hegemony.

Economic and technology considerations as well as social planning are the bases of much of the curriculum development and innovation today. The primacy of academic disciplines still reigns, and evaluative methods and measures remain largely unchanged from classical models used for centuries. As Truett and Doll (2010) acknowledge, "these practices produce and reproduce a culture" (p. 135).

Since the re-creation of a cultural mindset of some kind is all but certain (see Spring, 2007; Greene, 1988; Osberg and Biesta, 2010), it seems best to open a curriculum and its values to scrutiny, questioning, and dialogue rather than blindly or unconsciously replicating a given one or uncritically imposing some deliberate alternative. Scrutiny, questioning, dialogue, and conversation provide excellent opportunities to intellectualize content. For example, when David teaches the skills of representational drawing, he also brings into question the very ideas of representation, perception, and subject/object identity. When Sam introduces direct teaching and behavioral models, he places them in the context of what those models suggest about learning and has students compare those implications against contrasting cognitive research. As a result, students engage in intellectual scrutiny that informs the content. This allows a kind of curricular transcendence, if you will, where content is learned but also transcended. Skills are developed but perceived in a larger context, inevitably opening a space for conversation.

While scrutiny, questioning, and dialogue are useful intellectual processes, conversation personalizes content. In conversation, knowledge becomes personal and there is an existential quality to the information whereby decisions and choices are present. Ambiguity and creative tension show themselves in this arena and students are given space for complexity to enter where they can focus on both large and narrow concerns over time.

This is the space of emergence. This is the space where content becomes real because it is more a part of the students' lives. It is in the space of personal concern, ambiguity, collaborative insight, and emergent creativity where the curriculum—the manifest or imposed curriculum—disappears, perhaps not completely, but as a focal point. The focus, rather, is on the student's consolidated experience and how the student takes this into the world.

Curriculum as conversation (Applebee, 1996; Doll et al., 2005; Pinar, 2008) by its nature is subjective, nonlinear, process-oriented, iterative, experience-based, collaborative, and inherently creative. We are not suggesting that curriculum *is* conversation, rather that the idea of conversation is metaphorical.

When these attributes are applied to the question of curriculum it makes room for nonimpositional, more personalized, project-based learning. When extended over time and deepened with additional content, experience, observation, and yes, real conversation, it can also be transformative. When linked to larger human concerns and integrated into related content, a foundation for engaged service and personal responsiveness opens up.

Just as genuine conversation is emergent, in a similar way, a student interacts with content and creates personal or social applications that are truly constructivist in nature. Constructivism in a tightly controlled curriculum is an oxymoron.

Emergent teaching focuses on the student's experience rather than objectified content; thus the curriculum can be said to reside within the student. Then when guided, questioned, encouraged, and processed over time within a supportive community, curriculum emerges. From chaos and indeterminacy to determinate, consolidated understandings, it calls for response and application in the world. And thus a new space of emergence begins once again.

This focus on the learner is "holistic" in nature. We use this term perceptually rather than conceptually. This is because the *concept* of "wholeness" is elusive and problematic. Wholeness as a concept is all-inclusive and thus can never be observed from the outside, so it defies any definition that seeks to categorize or delineate it. However, as a *perceptual* term, one is challenged to connect rather than fragment, to see relationships rather than isolated entities, to understand dynamic interaction rather than static categories.

Perceptual wholeness is grounded in the idea of nonseparation discussed in depth in chapter 2. Therefore, this sense of perceptual holism places the human being within the larger context of experience where one seeks to understand the particular within a larger unity. Perceptual holism is consistent with emergent teaching and relates more practically to educators trying to understand holistic education.

Educators are beginning to respond to the idea that education must take seriously a more holistic perspective of the learner. Although a machine-oriented view of the world that sees things as fundamentally nondependent (separate, not connected) permeates our culture, there are too many scientific anomalies that suggest otherwise. And yet all social institutions, except those created in the last forty or fifty years, have been structured on machine-based assumptions (Goerner, 2001). And we continue to perpetuate those structural assumptions even though they no longer work for us.

These institutional configurations and the assumptions they are built upon simply cannot be sustained. Educators and professionals in other social institutions as well must either change the overall worldview of their institutions or create new institutions built upon radically different assumptions.

In the next section, a movement that reflects a more holistic perception of the learner is reviewed. Emergent teaching can provide a particularly useful and productive transition in which a perceptual perspective of wholeness can be implemented and explored.

TEACHING THE WHOLE PERSON

In education, there is a resurgent interest in the "whole child" as evidenced by a significant push by ASCD (Association For Supervision and Curriculum Development), one of the most influential of all educational associations, to promote a more expansive vision for America's schools. The emphasis on the whole child has endorsements from the American Association of School Administrators, the National Association of Elementary Principals, the National Association of Middle School Principals, and the National Association of Secondary School Principals, as well as from nearly every major professional organization dedicated to improving education.

While this emphasis is long overdue in education, there is little evidence thus far that there is a real understanding of how the mental, emotional, social, physical, environmental, and spiritual elements of a human being interact together or how to incorporate them holistically into educational design and educational culture. These developments are, however, clear indications of a general move away from perceiving education as a singular focus on mental development or, at the very least, toward understanding that intellectual development necessarily incorporates these additional aspects of human experience, just as physical health is enhanced by addressing these larger human needs.

To our knowledge, there are currently only two public universities in the United States that offer degrees in holistic education. The Masters in Holistic and Integrative Education at California State University, San Bernardino, has been in existence for over fifteen years and has an outstanding record of success. Many of the examples in this book come from the authors' experiences in this program.

A newer program at The Ohio State University offers a graduate option in holistic education. Outside the U.S., the prestigious University of Toronto/ OISE, through the leadership of Jack Miller, has played a major role in research and development of holistic perspectives and has also contributed to a growing interest in holistic programs throughout Europe and Asia. And Ramon Gallegos Nava in Mexico has developed both a masters' and doctoral program in holistic education.

There are, of course, private universities that have an emphasis on one or more of the six holistic aspects named above. Examples are the MA in Contemplative Teaching at Naropa University and the California Institute for Integral Studies. Dr. Aostre Johnson at St. Michael's College in Vermont directs a program in Spirituality and Education and sponsors courses and conferences that make research in this area available to the professional community.

Emergent teaching is naturally situated within the framework of the whole person and holistic education in general. While still an outlier in terms of its larger perspective, emergent teaching is relevant to the overall vision of the whole-child initiative and provides an additional lens on how to create educational experiences that are potentially transformative and significant for learners.

The overall context of emergent teaching is a teacher, classroom, or school that demonstrates a caring concern for the whole person. But what does this look like in concrete terms? The following discussion uses the six elements of holistic health to provide broad-brushed suggestions. The reader can use his or her own imagination and creativity to build upon these ideas. These six elements are interrelated and interwoven together. Indeed, the lack of fragmentation and the focus on relatedness are key signatures of holistic education. But of course the "whole person" does not exist any more than its fragments do. Rather it is merely a designation, a suggestion, that we are more (or perhaps less) than we appear to be. Wholeness, however it is defined, is actually part of our natural state.

The field of holistic health identifies six interactive elements that contribute to the well-being and health of an individual: the mental, emotional, social, physical, environmental, and spiritual conditions of life. These elements have been affirmed within the mainstream medical community even though they are not universally applied. While most medical research is clearly dedicated to the pathology of disease and the use of various drug interventions, more and more research on well-being and health maintenance finds the care of all six aspects to be essential to good health and overall happiness (e.g., Roizen and Oz, 2008).

Wholeness is a perspective that is grounded not only in our real experiences but also in a view of interconnection, relationship, and nonseparation. Therefore, it is instructive to apply the six elements used in holistic health to education. We will see that current and previous research already provides a firm foundation to perceive education more holistically. It also opens the door for additional research as well as new methods of inquiry that assist educators in transforming institutional assumptions and practices.

These six elements can be helpful in perceiving how human experience cannot be contained within any conceptual box. It is important to keep in mind that these holistic elements are not isolated categories but rather representative of interacting and interrelated human concerns.

MENTAL/INTELLECTUAL FOCUS

Most teachers have an obvious connection to the mental/intellectual focus of education and it could be argued that it comprises the central purpose of in-school learning. Whereas in the health profession the primary emphasis is on physiology and all other aspects support one's *physiological* well-being, one could say that for educators the central area of concern is mental and intellectual development, and the other elements of experience serve to enhance and support one's *intellectual* well-being. While this is certainly true, it nevertheless presents a mental trap of separating out one's experience into neatly defined categories and creating a working hierarchy of what is of greater or lesser importance.

Instead, we would like to look at the mental/intellectual aspect of experience from the point of view that it is inseparable from and cannot be defined in isolation from one's whole being. Neuropsychologist V. S. Ramachandran (2011), in discrediting a singular fragmented view of intelligence, observes that "no medical student who believed in 'general health' as a monolithic entity would get very far in medical school or be allowed to become a physician . . . and yet whole careers in psychology and political movements have been built on the equally absurd belief in single measurable general intelligence" (p. 171). The same holds true for educators. While learning necessarily involves mental and intellectual development, it is not limited to this category. If educators start with this assumption, the perception and definition of learning may become quite different from what it is today.

Rather than stress the importance of right answers and content information, intellectual development requires the ability to think, see patterns, consolidate understandings, and make applications (Bruner, 2006; Piaget, 2001; Steinberg, 2010). Educators need to once and for all reject the view that learning is primarily tied to information processing and memory; this simply is not true. Yet most instructional efforts and evaluations are structured around this false assumption.

Education will not improve until the focus of instruction changes to include a more intellectual, physically engaging, and creative purpose. This point has been confirmed by research for at least half a century but given the societal expectations and political/economic pressures, schools have not been able to successfully restructure their emphasis on a large scale.

Caine and Caine (1991) have synthesized studies from the neurosciences for more than two decades and have demonstrated that in the simplest of terms the function of the brain is to make sense of one's experience. Subsequently, the executive function of the cerebral cortex is to *apply* one's perceptual understanding in the real world. Perception and action constitute a single response system (Fuster, 2008; Caine and Caine, 2011). To provide authentic opportunities that serve students' mental and intellectual development requires a new mindset and supportive structures.

Emergent teaching can be helpful in making this transition. As part of a more holistic perspective, emergent teaching engages the student in genuine and personal inquiry *over time* where patterns can be recognized, changes and subtleties can be examined, and deepening conversation and questioning can be encouraged. In emergent teaching, natural extensions can be explored and applications can be related to personal interests and identified needs. Mental and intellectual growth blossoms in this kind of invitational yet rigorous atmosphere.

EMOTIONAL FOCUS

The link between emotion and cognition has been understood by almost anyone who has been in the classroom on a daily basis working with children. But scientific theory for most of the twentieth century neatly separated these out as if they were unrelated. It wasn't that teachers did not deal with students' emotional issues; it was just that emotion and cognitive development were treated separately.

Even as Bloom (1984) offered his cognitive, affective, and psychomotor domains as interrelated concepts, the education community continued to treat them separately, with only a hint that they were indivisible, holistic aspects of cognitive functioning. It wasn't until research from the neurosciences demonstrated that all experience, including thinking, contains emotional content for the learner that the educational community began thinking seriously about including emotional development as part of its purpose.

Emotional content consists of personalized, individual responses based on previous experiences or internalized perceptions (Caine et al., 1999; Damasio, 1999; Siegel, 2012). Anything learned is emotionally processed by the learner and as a result carries with it emotional content.

In addition, research on the impact of stress on learning (Schiering et al., 2011; Childre et al., 2000) opened up new and important understandings that can be applied effectively in classrooms to help students enjoy the experience of learning with less fear and anxiety. Stress not only reduces the effectiveness of memory systems but it also negatively affects an individual's ability for creative problem-solving.

However, most classrooms operate on the basis that stress is good, that it "toughens" you, that it prepares students for life in society. In fact, stress is the number one source of illness and death (Sapolsky, 2004). Overall, it works against learning. Yes, moderate stress represented as challenge is a positive and engaging attribute. But stress characterized by fear, worry, anxiety, and helplessness leads to severe physical and mental disabilities. Educators often unwittingly create conditions of helplessness with assignment overload, high-stakes competitive testing, and deadlines that are inflexible and based on pacing guides and other mandates.

Emotional distress can also come from impersonal or depersonalized classrooms, a lack of community, a sense of not belonging, or seemingly irrelevant content that does not speak to students' interests or needs but nevertheless has high expectations or conversely very little expectation that some students can succeed.

When students are not provided the skills they need to deal constructively with interpersonal issues, when they feel diminished or under threat of being bullied, the emotional context is not conducive for learning. When students have difficulty understanding the language or culture of the school community, they can feel easily defeated or unworthy.

Trust, safety, the right to make and correct mistakes, the genuine support of caring adults, and an atmosphere of communication are essential characteristics for emotional stability. Practices that teach how to manage stress, opportunities to talk with others and collaborate, and time to allow one's understanding to unfold all support students' emotional needs. When students recognize that their emotions are tied to learning, they develop more awareness of themselves, their goals, and personal strengths and positive attributes as well.

Emergent teaching, as developed in the previous chapters, fully addresses the emotional aspect of the whole person and makes it a central consideration of the teacher/student relationship. There is a level of acceptance of the student for who they are that is accentuated in the pedagogy of emergence. The subjective experience of learning is accentuated and the lived experience of the learner is valued.

When the conditions for emotional safety are extended to the larger classroom environment, a teacher can feel the difference. The internal and external elements form a natural unity that affects everything else—and everybody. This is a physiological fact (Childre et al., 2000). And the emotional climate extends naturally to influence and affect the social context of the classroom.

THE SOCIAL FOCUS

Part of the emphasis in this book has been a focus on complex adaptive open systems where there is a dynamic web of interactions and reciprocal relationships. Emergence happens within this kind of environment. A holistic perspective necessarily includes an emphasis on the social environment. Human beings are social creatures.

Goerner (2001) reminds us that "living organisms are not separate, they co-evolve with the larger whole" (p. 185). This understanding should make it obvious that one of the educator's key tasks is the establishment of community and a strong sense of belonging. The recent work in social neurobiology (Cozolino, 2008; Siegel, 2010) confirms the importance of a caring and productive social/emotional context.

Educational research over the years has addressed the sociocultural nature of learning and the significance of community, interaction, and play (Vygotsky, 1978; Wertsch, 1998; Friere, 1970; Wink, 2010). Even the more existential aspects of learning require an awareness of one's place within a societal context. Greene (1988) developed this concept beautifully as she examined freedom as inherently tied to one's participation within a community and the public sphere.

Schools today that seek to emphasize teaching the whole child are often structured around "communities" of learners in which teachers try to create programs and strategies that address the specific needs and concerns of their students. When these "communities" are merely organizational formats having little to do with social development and building a true sense of community, they are largely ineffectual. But when there is a serious attempt to build a genuine family of learners and where teachers play important and integral roles in creating opportunities for relationship, the conditions that foster student success are a natural outcome (Samaras, Freese, Kosnic, and Beck eds., 2008; Larrivee, 2008).

The vast majority of schools ignore the power and possibility of the social self. Classrooms are organized around a direct model of transmission that inhibits and squelches learner interaction. Most management approaches also are based on the assumption of direct teaching. In addition, school scheduling and time delimitations reinforce it. Still further, pacing guides and curriculum coverage expectations assume transmission-oriented instruction that is too often inconsistent with mastery learning.

Authentic communities require genuine interaction and collaboration. Project-based learning, for example, to be effective, needs a social environment that teaches how to work collaboratively and productively (Schlemmer and Schlemmer, 2008). Emergent teaching recognizes the social nature of learning. In the stories we have relayed, students worked both individually and collaboratively. Personal accountability merged with group creativity. Not only did students find this work challenging, they were invigorated by the interaction. For us, it was the processing of students' experience that helped to create a safe space where individuals could be heard and trust could be established. It was also through the processing of experience that understandings could be deepened and bridges to conceptual content could be established.

Creating a positive social climate does not mean that a teacher does group work all the time. Even during lectures, having students periodically pair up to spend one or two minutes discussing insights or asking questions enlivens a class and invites participation. Giving students opportunities for genuine decision-making engages them in the things that concern them and offers a way to extend learning to the wider community.

Emergent teaching helps a teacher establish an ongoing narrative in which the classroom culture becomes an unseen teacher, where stories and lived experience become significant partners for learning, and where the invisible hand of culture emerges through the chaos and complexity of real life. Viewing social interaction from the point of view of a complex adaptive open system provides a wide array of insights for the teacher. The social nature of learning is real. It is an important aspect of a holistic approach to education.

PHYSIOLOGICAL FOCUS

At its heart, all learning is physiological (Crowell et al., 2001). This book has already suggested that neural processes are not limited to the brain mass contained inside the human skull but rather are distributed throughout the body in an extensive network of electrochemical activity. In fact, neurons, just like those found in the brain, are also found in the heart and in the gut (Childre and Martin, 2000). The human nervous system is comprised of neural bundles that are constantly interacting with the entire physiology, mostly without one's conscious awareness. We process, integrate, and act upon information with our bodies. Learning is physiological.

The assumption that the most efficient learning occurs in a hermetic environment where there are no distractions contains two fallacies: first, that human physiology is only a closed system, and second, that learning is most efficient and significant when it is limited by subject matter presented in small bits and pieces.

The current model of education is based on the premise that learning is about regurgitating facts and teaching is about delivering content. This model is often compared to an assembly line of a factory where teachers are like assembly line workers who are expected to deposit the same information to every student in the same way as fast as they can. In this model, information is disembodied and held in the head. The result is that both students and teachers feel disempowered, information is standardized, and students are treated as empty containers with little or no agency.

By contrast, a holistic approach to education affirms that human beings are open systems and as such constantly receive many different kinds of information in many different ways and on a variety of different levels. In the animal world, consider the way starlings form undulating, swirling clouds of collective awareness. These murmurations, as they are called, are a form of knowing that is rooted in their physiology. This kind of somatic or bodily knowing is less obvious in our own behaviors, unless circumstances override the intellectual response. But somatic and autonomic systems are continuously operating within the human body.

A clear but disturbing example of how the body receives and stores information is illustrated in the story of a friend who came from an abusive family. When she was a young girl her father got drunk and tried to physically abuse her. She tried desperately to fend him off but he overwhelmed her by hitting her on the nose and knocking her out. Forty years later she was undergoing therapy when she had a flashback of this traumatic event, and almost immediately her nose started bleeding. What this example demonstrates is the ability of the body to hold information. It calls into question the notion that memory is only held in the brain, and by implication that the brain is the only organ that learns.

When the body/mind is viewed as an inseparable whole and physiology is included in instructional decisions, then even though outcomes may be less predictable, learning nevertheless becomes emergent and fulfilling. This is because individuals process physical experience (as well as all other kinds of experience) differently. Incorporating physicality into the learning process opens up an interesting diversity of meanings and reflections. It also raises the level of engagement and seems to increase memory.

Sitting still for long periods of time without moving is an obstacle to learning. The body is not meant to be stationary; it is meant to move. Research indicates that even minimal movement (like standing up, taking three steps forward and three steps back, then sitting down again) every twenty minutes improves concentration, memory, and attention (Medina, 2009). Physical experience provides an embodied way to understand content, especially when a bridge between experience and concept is provided (Zull, 2002; Zull, 2011).

Many teachers, however, are afraid of the management difficulties involved in activity-based experiences. While physicality suggests movement, hands-on activity, and experiential learning, it does not have to be a daunting production. Just remember that at the heart of physiology and learning is the human sensory system.

Using multiple modalities that engage the sight, hearing, taste, smell, and touch enhance any teacher's repertoire. Providing reasons, explaining procedures, and setting boundaries are no different from any other teaching activity. Teachers in science labs, shop, studio art, band, and theater are ideal resources to learn how to incorporate more physical activity into the learning process of any classroom or subject area. They do it every day. Preschools or kindergarten classes are also excellent models for an embodied approach to instruction.

As explored throughout these chapters, the attributes of nonlinearity, process, creativity, consolidation, indeterminate outcome, coevolution, subjective meaning, and transformation all occur in art and in nature. A physiological focus in which embodied learning is an essential characteristic of human experience is integral to one's humanity. Perceiving mind/body as an interrelated system is an important key to teaching the whole person.

ENVIRONMENTAL FOCUS

Educators have always been interested in creating positive learning environments for students. Many efforts in the past, however, focused more on decoration than on creating a dynamic, integrated, multifaceted context for learning. This is not to say that aesthetically pleasing classrooms are not important. It is only to acknowledge that the whole person necessarily includes the environment. Humans learn from their surroundings and the totality of one's experience becomes literally and biologically part of the person. Emergence takes place in a complex, multilayered context. Therefore, the mental, emotional, social, and physiological factors cannot be separate from place. Whether or not one accepts the theory of enactive cognition (Varela, Thompson, and Rosch, 1991; Shapiro, 2010), situatedness and the role of the environment are undeniable factors of what make us human. There is no experience without place.

Research in neurobiology raises fascinating new questions concerning the biological impact of the environment on DNA, neural processing, and cognitive development (Zull, 2011; Doidge, 2007). Environmental factors can biologically alter the brain. The age-old argument of nature vs. nurture is not even a relevant question anymore. It is scientifically naïve to even consider such a division. In addition, research over the past thirty years confirms commonsense notions that an enriched environment has powerful implications for brain development. The research goes still further to indicate that experiential learning environments create the largest positive effect on learning (Diamond and Hopson, 1999; Caine and Caine, 2011).

It may be helpful to think of the environment in two distinct ways. The first is the physical space itself; the second is what happens in the space. In general, physical space for learning should be multisensory and flexible.

Human beings respond to the environment through the senses. Over the years, studies have shown that certain kinds of music, art, and fragrance are stimulating, particularly when altered periodically to produce novelty and change. The RAS (reticular activating system), found in the human brain stem, responds to new or interesting changes in the environment and other parts of the brain activate to process various kinds of experience (Jensen, 2007; Evanshen and Faulk, 2011).

While overstimulation can be a problem for some students, more typically when a teacher orchestrates the learning environment around key activities and purposes, positive results are attained. Teaching the whole person requires the educator to incorporate a wide array of environmental understandings to create an integrative context for learning.

Emergent teaching goes further, in that it brings attention to these kinds of environmental factors as multiple layers of experience. Structuring complexity makes the environment a more conscious and integral aspect of a student's experience, to be processed and understood, not in isolation but in connection to what is being consolidated and learned. Emergent teaching sets up opportunities for "something to happen."

Interaction with the environment is purposeful and the learner participates in it in some way. An awareness of personal feelings, choices, responses, and new understandings is encouraged so that outcomes are dependent, tentative, and foundational. Emergent teaching incorporates the sensibility of chaos and complexity into the learning experience. The environment is never isolated; it is both the container for what happens as well as the context for what emerges.

There is a Chinese proverb that says a house is comprised of walls, windows, and doors but it is the empty space inside where living occurs. This is an apt metaphor for thinking about the environment. The environment is not a static concept. It holistically integrates the aspects of the whole person previously discussed: mental/intellectual, emotional, social, and physiological. Furthermore, it would be a mistake to view the "environment" as restricted to the classroom or school. Interaction with the larger community, the virtual community, and nature brings life to learning. It provides opportunities to apply, to experiment, to gain perspective, to serve. When the environment is perceived in terms of situated experience, as a place where learning happens, where caring, trust, and community are nurtured, where belonging, interaction, and collaboration are fostered, and where creativity, play, movement, and participation are encouraged, then the environment comes to life and becomes an integral partner in the educational process.

THE SPIRITUAL FOCUS

There is yet another element that is perceived as essential to holistic health. It is an element that is generally ignored in education due to its association with religion and a fear that students will have beliefs and dogmas imposed or forced upon them. This is the spiritual dimension of the human experience. These are legitimate concerns. So how can educators address this significant aspect of our humanity in ways that are appropriate and in ways that enhance learning?

We humans throughout our history have focused on questions regarding the significance of life and the meaning of existence—how to live, how to interact with one another, how to treat others, how to cultivate the best in ourselves so that we might live a life of meaning and purpose. These questions were situated within the fabric of a community; there was a sense of connection with others, with origins, with the narratives and stories of a people. There was also a connection with the natural world and with a felt sense of mystery and awe. To experience this connection was to be happy, to understand one's purpose, to be an extension of the wonder of creation.

The idea of spirit is centered in the animating, unseen forces of life. The word "spirit" literally means *breath*. Breath is something that all humans have in common. Without breath there is no life. To be in the presence of a person who has taken their last breath is to realize that life is indeed a gift, and every time one exhales, there is no certainty that another breath will come.

So the word "spirit" has its roots in signifying what is most important in life. And with it there is a sense of gratitude for being alive and an urgency to pursue a life of purpose and integrity. Finding this sense of purpose and cultivating a good life create questions of ultimate concern that have to be discovered for oneself. These are heart-based questions in the sense that they can only be explored from within. One's inner life is an essential aspect of a person's overall development and happiness as a human being.

Without a sense of purpose and meaning, learning has very little significance. Moore (1992) poignantly addressed the lack of meaning and connection in today's world:

> As long as we leave care of the soul out of our daily lives we will suffer the loneliness of living in a dead, cold, unrelated world. We can 'improve' ourselves to the maximum, and yet we will still feel the alienation inherent in a divided existence. We will continue to exploit nature and our capacity to invent new things, but both will continue to overpower us, if we do not approach them with enough depth and imagination. (p. 282)

This lack of real connection to the world around us, to one another, and to ourselves is emblematic of a modernist worldview that characterizes our time. It is a crisis of separation in which the universe is largely perceived as devoid of meaning, where nature is treated in terms of isolated entities and nondependent objects (Berman, 1981; Gablik, 2002).

This thinking represents the view of a fragmented reality in which independent and isolated parts are merely constitutive elements that have no significance beyond their immediate deterministic function. Berman (1981) refers to this mentality as disenchantment.

This disenchanted worldview has consequences. Even if individuals don't personally share this perspective of the world, each one of us is affected by it. This view of separation characterizes all of our primary institutions and lies at the foundation of how most of our global societies define problems and approach solutions.

The fact is, schools replicate and reify this worldview by focusing on fragmented information in fragmented subjects in fragmented time blocks with little or no sense of continuity, connectivity, or relatedness. Most of the content is presented devoid of meaning and significance and there is little attempt to relate it to the personal lives of students. Therefore, the focus of education continues to be on the external—on what is observable and measurable. Education has abandoned the inner world and inner life of students and has thus lost the *breath*, the life-force, of what learning is meant to be.

This crisis of meaning and ways to address it are discussed in length in *The Re-Enchantment of Learning* (Crowell et al., 2001). The purpose here is to point out that there is a natural quest for meaning, purpose, and significance that is largely unaddressed in society and ignored by its institutions. One's inner life is the driving force of the whole person.

Recently, there has been considerable interest from educators and researchers seeking to explore how to address the spiritual dimension of students' lives in public settings (Miller, 2011; Miller, 2005; Collister 2010; Rendon, 2009; Glazer, ed., 1999). These works have little or nothing to do with religion.

Aostre Johnson (2011), who has researched this area for many years, has identified seven capacities that can be developed by educators: (1) the capacity for awareness, concentration, and contemplation; (2) the capacity to internalize and process what is personally meaningful; (3) the ability to self-reflect; (4) the emotional capacity to experience a sense of wonder, awe, love, gratitude, and joy; (5) the capacity to develop ethical values that influence one's actions and responsibilities; (6) an ecological capacity that perceives a sense of place and a connection with nature; and (7) the capacity for creative expression and imagination. When teachers incorporate these capacities in their teaching, students have a greater connection to the learning. It relates to what is really important.

Psychologist Tobin Hart (2011) also writes of the heightened potential of learning when students are invited to nourish their inner lives. He shifts attention away from what one knows or how one learns to *how* one knows. Hart is concerned with depth and significance, what he calls *intimate knowing*. This designation is more akin to the cultivation of wisdom. It is the kind of knowing that has transformative potential (Hart, 2009). Transformation has an inner locus of control.

Biologist James Zull (2011) uses a scientific understanding of the brain to make a similar point. He deepens the concept of metacognition by emphasizing the reflective processing of our interior world—not just how a problem is solved or delineating a thought process. Zull goes further by emphasizing awareness and insight and, as other neuroscientists are beginning to do, he distinguishes between brain and mind.

A spiritual focus is an important consideration in teaching the whole person. It means *breathing life* into the curriculum and infusing the learning process with the wonder and awe of content, with the joy of living and the significance of possibility. It connects the external and internal worlds as natural partners in the search for meaning and incorporates imagination and creativity as essential characteristics of life's journey.

Emergent teaching very much engages the inner life of students. Throughout this book we have introduced stories that point to the importance of inner experience in transformative learning. As iterated throughout the chapters, emergent teaching creates layers of complex experience and creative chaos that require consolidation and processing. Students are not separate from the learning experience; their lives are integral to whatever outcomes emerge.

If there is a latent or hidden curricular message in emergent teaching, it is the perception that the world does not exist in separate, isolated categories. And because humans live in a nonseparate universe, there is an inevitable connection with the natural world, society, one another, and one's inner experience. Our students will often refer to this sense of connection as "spiritual." But there is no overt attempt to characterize it in that way. However, when one feels connected, there is a sense of expansion, of belonging, of being a part of something larger than oneself.

In our experience, this sense of connection is enhanced most in the communities we established with our students, in the opportunities for them to engage in creative and imaginative play, and in learning and working together in nature. Students saw the natural interconnectedness in these experiences that they internalized in very distinctive and unique ways. We invited contemplation and provided opportunities for students to take the gift of themselves into the world and to allow their sense of purpose and their heartfelt interests to keep emerging. For us, emergent teaching has redefined our own life-worlds, purposes, and commitments. In the process of creating emergent and transformative experiences for our students, it is we who have been transformed.

Chapter Ten

The Path of Emergence in the Classroom

Emergent teaching is not a methodology. This kind of teaching is not formulaic; it resists prediction and control, hence the significance of story, reflection, and sharing through conversation. We have not set out to describe a formalized approach to instruction. Rather, this book has been an inquiry into the concept of emergence in terms of a deep reflection on real experience. Emergence is nature's creative process and is integral to chaos and complexity theory.

But what does emergence mean for educators? How can we teachers understand complexity theories in terms of educational practice? How does emergence challenge our assumptions about teaching and learning? And how does emergence inform educators' perception of creativity and transformation?

In this section, we will share our personal suggestions for implementing emergent teaching into the classroom. We intend this to be a conversation with the reader with the hope that our comments will initiate new questions and interests.

If I were to implement emergent teaching into my classroom, what would be some first steps?

We would start by infusing the students' perspectives and experiences into the content. Co-ownership of the educational experience is an important way to build trust, create conversation, and build community. For us, we try to communicate to our students early on that there will be a shift in focus from the curriculum to the learner. Shifting this focus creates opportunities for students to be more engaged and teachers to be more naturally responsive.

For example, students in Sam's writing class are treated as writers, not as students. Challenges, fears, and hopes are honored as part of the writing process and part of the general conversation about writing. Each person is committed to helping the others become better writers. The class becomes more of a writers' studio where certain skills or ideas are emphasized but everyone is at a different place. The content comes directly out of the students' needs and questions. Trust and confidence tend to be natural outcomes. A sense of trust and community is essential to be able to make emergent opportunities work in the classroom. Shifting the focus to the students is a first step to natural emergence.

Both of us also spend a lot of time thinking about the importance of ritual and environment and how to create opportunities for students to collaborate. David creates activities where students share assignments. Sometimes he will have students combine their individual work to create something new and original. Sam has students review the previous class and add their own thoughts and questions in order to reconstruct what is relevant to them.

It is important to remember that emergence requires a degree of uncertainty or interaction. These small bursts of creative chaos can usually be structured and accommodated in most classrooms. The room and the community become an active organism that is full of energy and possibility. Emergence then happens on its own!

How does a teacher deal with fear and uncertainty in an emergent environment?

We have found that to occupy the space of uncertainty is similar to improvisation. When we are improvising we are focused and present, open and receptive. The more we do this the more exciting and fun it becomes. Of course there are some initial fears, but we are conditioned to think we have to have all the answers and that any kind of disruption is bad. However, the fulfillment of seeing students invested and engaged overrides one's initial fears and gives a degree of confidence to continue.

Also, just like improvisation, there are rules and boundaries. These need to be appropriate to the task or activity. Problems that arise are not necessarily bad, because they provide new opportunities for learning. Our own stories have shown that some of the most transformative moments emerged out of unanticipated problems. It was through processing these with our students that new layers of emergence were created. Fear is probably inevitable, but it diminishes with time and does not have to be debilitating.

How can I use emergent teaching in an environment that is focused only on specific outcomes and measurable achievements?

While the two of us use various emergent practices in every class and as a model for how we think about teaching and learning, we understood when we began this book that most teachers and school administrators are not given the freedom to work outside a predetermined set of curricular expectations. Nor are they allowed to develop innovative instructional pedagogies that fall too far from the norm.

This kind of restriction is a type of reverse coercion in which innovation and professional integrity become squelched or compromised. Real innovation never happens under such conditions. However, in every classroom and every school there are spaces where new approaches can be applied, either inside or outside a curriculum.

We think that for teachers, using long-term parallel emergent assignments that are extensions of the curriculum is a practical place to begin. Or teachers may wish to work individually with certain students who show interests and needs outside the prescribed expectations.

For schools, we suggest using a thematic focus that becomes a long-term parallel meta-curriculum in which all teachers and students participate. Creating a school-wide focus that permeates the whole school culture and can be explored within every subject matter from a unique perspective is an exciting way to create emergence.

For example, establishing a year-long theme like "Honoring the Diversity in Our World" with a culminating week of sharing and celebration, speakers and special events, service and project-based research can infuse the entire school with new energy and open a space for emergent teaching throughout the year. Diversity can be treated broadly as it relates to culture, nature, personality, inclusion, individual talents and gifts, and so on, even differential equations. Students, as well as teachers, can collaborate, follow interests and inquiries, and create subjective, personalized responses and art.

A group of schools could collaborate on common themes, with networked inquiries and projects where students engage together and communicate virtually across or within subject matter or grade levels. Possibilities are only limited by imagination.

We think the Earth Charter can be a great source for identifying significant, purposeful themes or guiding the larger discussions, especially the four broad categories of Respect for Diversity, Ecological Integrity, Social and Economic Justice, and Peace, Nonviolence, and Democracy. These themes lend themselves to being repeated every four years with new energy and new students providing increasing layers of complexity and emergence.

Emergent teaching works especially well with a parallel meta-curriculum that engages layered complexity and creative chaos. While this kind of parallel theme can be developed in any classroom, when it pervades an entire school culture, there is a vitality and sense of community that can be felt. Importantly, this type of focus creates a context for staff development through conversation and process.

Establishing the conditions for emergence allows a school staff to occupy that space, share stories of success and frustration, follow as well as lead, and learn to trust the process. Professional development then occurs out of need and interests and the opportunity to establish trust in one another.

Emergent teaching is possible even when the rest of the curriculum is constrained and limited. In fact, it is our experience that such environments become less constrained when teachers observe the natural excitement, engagement, and meaningful participation of the students. Also, there is a spillover effect into the regular curriculum and the instructional process.

When teachers feel more comfortable with emergent teaching, they naturally find ways to incorporate it into the established curriculum (see Crowell and Caine in Jennings ed., 1997). Emergent teaching is a pedagogical approach that is flexible and adaptive as well as uniquely individual. It resists the familiar mass consumption of instructional methodology. It is a mind shift that has a pervasive influence on the entire context.

Finally, it is worth noting that there is increasing interest in charter schools, innovative teacher-owned schools, private/independents, and other nonconventional learning centers. Emergent teaching offers these environments a new mindset for instruction and for a student-oriented "curriculum that disappears."

How do I create assignments that are emergent?

Assignments in emergent teaching may have criteria that relate to the development of certain skills or presentation requirements, but these tend to be less rigid than in other types of assignments. As a whole, emergent assignments stay away from point systems and detailed rubrics.

The idea is to provide boundaried freedom that encourages students to explore their own thinking, develop new skills or perspectives, and provides opportunities to present information, experience, or products in creative, original ways. The focus is on what is happening within the student rather than a content outcome. Yet often it is *through* the content outcome that we get insight into the student's inner world.

Teachers may find it useful to think of assignments in emergent teaching as having two characteristics: (1) layered complexity and (2) creative chaos. Layered complexity means that assignments become layered over time. They begin with simplicity, and through sharing and processing are taken to deeper, more complex levels. The more something is shared, consolidated, and extended the more complex it becomes. Creative chaos refers to participating in nonlinear processes that create the need for synthesis or consolidation.

For example, a closing course activity that Sam sometimes uses is having students review notes, readings, assignments, lectures, class activities, and group discussions in order to write a reflective essay that consolidates what was most significant for them, how what they learned relates to the field or to their interests, and how specifically they intend to apply or use what they learned.

Students share this written assignment in small groups and then are asked to consolidate the various reflections as a group and to creatively present this to the class. The following week each group makes an original presentation that is then processed and celebrated as a whole class. Layered complexity and creative chaos are both apparent in this assignment and the final result is emergent and beyond prediction.

The final presentations are equally enjoyable and profound. Somehow, the students take their experience beyond the confines of the course as they interject their own personalities, questions, and interests into their reflections. Something original and unexpected always emerges.

The assignment just described has many of the features that were emphasized in the previous chapters of the book. The *processes* used in this assignment built upon *nonlinearity*. There were multiple *iterations* of content and experience throughout the assignment. *Subjective meaning* and significance were emphasized and honored. *Personal* accountability (the individual papers were turned in separately) as well as *interaction* and *collaboration* were woven together. The outcome was continuously tentative and *evolving*; the assignment became increasingly *complex* and yet never lost its inherent simplicity. Embedded in the culmination was an emphasis on *imagination* and *creative expression* that was challenging but playful. The whole assignment began with *what was most important* to the student and in the end asked how their knowledge and understandings could be taken *into the world*. The final celebration included *ritual* and *ceremony* that engaged the entire *community*.

Sam often concludes the class with a few words of gratitude and a poem like this one by Stephanie Chase.

> Children of the Earth,
> Come out of the darkness—
> Light your candles from the stars . . .
> Keep vigil for all the world.
> Let no heart deny the other,
> Let your love be the sign of peace
> Made visible.

Beyond the course and beyond the content, *transformation* and *possibility* still lie ahead. There are other things to keep in mind when creating emergent assignments. It sometimes helps to frame them as questions.

- Is the assignment open-ended?
- Does it include the student's subjective experience?
- Are there collaborative opportunities involved?
- Is it experiential, physical, or interactive?
- How will the assignment be processed?
- Does it include opportunities to be creative?
- Does it involve a change in the environment?
- Does it have impact on the larger community?
- Does it encourage personal choices and responses?
- Is there a consolidation or culmination?

All of these characteristics do not have to be a part of every emergent assignment, and you may want to add your own. But these questions provide a way to think about the processes and layers of activity a teacher may wish to include.

From our experience, it helps to have a degree of dialogue about the assignment at the beginning. We suggest that a teacher spend some time explaining the purpose of the assignment and giving enough guidance for students to feel secure but not too much so that they feel constrained.

Emergent assignments are built upon trust and if students don't feel safe in going their own way, emergent teaching will not work. Of course, feeling insecure is an excellent topic for discussion and provides a forum to explore the obstacles to learning. We have found that it is also important to periodically check in with students to see what they are doing, share their ideas, provide additional guidance, or make suggestions.

Sometimes students also need to be taught certain skills that are relevant to the assignment. Another variation used by David is to use blind critiques with other students. For example, he will occasionally enlist other classes to provide feedback to anonymous projects at some midway point. Students can then use this information to refine or rethink what they are doing. Another way to invigorate the project is to somehow alter the environment. It may be by going outside, visiting a community site that relates to the assignment, or having guests come to the classroom.

The space of emergence is where openness, interaction, and unpredictability are allowed to converge. What results is the natural unfolding of complexity and chaos. Inhabiting this space is emergent teaching.

What qualities seem to be important in emergent teaching and how can they be cultivated?

Qualities that support emergence can vary from person to person, but from our experience certain attributes seem particularly helpful and are worthy of cultivation. Among these we would list being flexible and adaptive, creative, inclusive, open, and playful. These qualities together help the teacher create an atmosphere of engagement and joy. They allow the teacher to respond in the moment and occupy that space of uncertainty and nonlinearity that characterizes emergence.

Other important qualities include nonjudgmental acceptance, empathetic listening, kindness and caring, open-minded questioning, and trusting self and others. Because emergent teaching emanates from within, this cluster of qualities provides students the self-confidence to engage in their own journey of uncertainty and discovery, knowing the teacher is by their side.

The generality of these qualities is intentional. They are meant to be defined in the context of one's experience and within a community of discourse. They are not presented as ideals or directives but come out of our own reflections and conversations.

In terms of cultivating these attributes we have found that we need to have some kind of creative practice that strengthens our own inner resources and prepares us to live a more emergent life. For David this is his art; for Sam, it is poetry. The teachers we teach also begin to discover or re-engage in some kind of creative endeavor. It seems to recharge a child-like joy that energizes the spirit and is deeply satisfying. Creativity places one in the midst of process and nonlinearity and goes to the heart of who we are as human beings.

For us, it is also important to make time for quietude and contemplation. This might be in the form of journaling or flow-of-consciousness writing. It might be sitting quietly in the backyard listening intently to the birds begin their day, or silently contemplating an inspiring quotation. Such nonactivity tends to draw us inward and let us focus on the simplicities of life or on what is most important to us.

Both of us are long-time meditators. While our meditative practice is informed by different traditions, both of us feel that meditation should not be heavily governed by rules or laden with idealizations that are projected and generated by wish fulfillment. Meditation for us is simply a time to become aware of the natural movement of one's mind. This may lead to focused and cultivated experiences, but it begins with receptive awareness. In meditation, one experiences the mind as both full and empty. It pays attention and it wanders. It is agitated and it is unbelievably peaceful. It analyzes and it has flashes of insight. It experiences oblivion and it transports one to a rapturous joy. It inspires and directs as well as reveals and perplexes. It is deeply emotional and yet can be strangely impersonal. Meditation somehow invites a deeper understanding of both our conditioning and our possibilities.

The value of meditation is found in the details and particularities of one's own experience, not a prearranged set of concepts. The two of us have developed a greater connection to our own inner worlds and we feel more connected to the world we inhabit. For us, meditation is a time of retreat, of understanding, of inner nourishment. It really does make a difference.

In terms of cultivating qualities for emergent teaching, meditation is an amazing example of emergence in action. One begins to create within oneself a greater tolerance for ambiguity and an increased understanding of the depth and capacity of the mind to act upon and consolidate itself. We introduce meditation to our graduate students who have found it to be a respite in their daily lives, accompanied by a greater sense of purpose and insight into the issues that concern them.

We have also found that various kinds of discipline-based physiological activity have surprising benefits apart from physical and mental health. Sam has a daily practice of tai chi and chi gong, which are referred to as inner martial arts. Both of these engage the mind and body. Over the years these practices have become active metaphors for emergence—constant movement, repeating patterns, balance and flexibility, internal and external integration, concentrated attention, and awareness.

David, besides doing very physical sculptural projects, is sought after for his landscaping rock creations. He works organically, helping each rock find its natural place. He becomes physically and mentally engrossed in the process and activates his intuition throughout the project.

An activity might be yoga, Pilates, dance, gardening, running, or biking. In each of these one can discover the tangible metaphors and life lessons that emerge when we lose ourselves in discipline-based physical activity. And life becomes a laboratory for our teaching.

For us, nothing is so full of examples of emergence as the natural world. Spending time in nature restores and refreshes us from the inside out. It invites the development of so many of the qualities important for emergent teaching. Many refer to our ecological self as one of the least developed aspects of the modern experience. Our disconnection from nature is one of the sad conditions of our time. In the modern experience it is possible to wake up, go to work, run errands, enjoy entertainment, go home, and go to bed without ever encountering the natural world. And this can happen day after day.

When we conduct some of our masters' classes at a wilderness retreat, we notice that our students' whole demeanor changes. Year after year each group describes the experience in nature as one of the most nurturing aspects of the program. When Sam took students to experience the natural beauty of

Costa Rica, they later described it as a life-altering and unforgettable trip. When we are in nature our entire physiology is affected. There is some kind of interchange that can be felt at a subtle level of our being (see Buhner, 2004; Plotkin, 2007). It can be a park, a garden, or just a seat under a tree.

For the two of us, being in nature is not optional; it is an integral part of life. David places himself purposefully within nature every day, and Sam hikes two to three times a week. Being in nature feeds the sense of connection and relationship that spills over into other areas of life. Simplicities and complexities are found everywhere, and life as event is illustrated at every turn. Even in a city there are opportunities to seek out and establish a connection with the natural world.

Finally, the two of us feel that regular conversations over time reveal many of the principles of emergence, but more importantly they become a basis for friendship and support. Trust, authenticity, patience, listening, empathy, and appreciation are often natural outcomes of long-term conversation; at least they were for us.

It is difficult to immerse oneself in a new pedagogical approach alone. When there is a friend who both listens and shares the successes and disappointments that are inevitable, it provides the courage and inspiration to continue. We believe, based not only on our experience but also on research on institutional change, that the seeds of emergent energy embedded in focused conversation over time unfold a process for both personal and professional transformation.

Developing practices that nourish the inner life affects the whole of one's being. When educators engage in these kinds of self-nurturance, it will also make a difference in the classroom. Seeing the world from a new perspective makes everything new and original. Possibility emerges from within and manifests itself in everything one does.

How can emergent teaching be a part of professional development?

Our view of most professional development is that even under good circumstances it is largely a fragmented process—some new methodology comes down the pike and teachers are forced to learn it, or, perhaps more often, a new structural component is proposed and teachers are introduced to it and given implementation time. An example of the new methodology might be project-based learning; an example of the structural component could be professional learning communities or PLCs.

Too often the ongoing processes and commitments that support real professional growth are not put into place. So teachers end up spending enormous amounts of time and energy revving up for something that will not be cultivated substantively and supported over time. This leads to both emotional and financial waste and a lack of real innovation or reform.

Creating positive conditions for professional development, however, can invigorate and inspire an entire staff. We think the works of Klimak et al. in *Generative Leadership* (2008) and Schwahn and Spady in *Total Leaders* (2002) are excellent resources for this. The latter identifies five pillars of change that are essential: purpose, vision, ownership, capacity, and support. Most professional development, however, is directed only at capacity, or the building of technical knowledge.

But just as in the everyday classroom, information alone rarely leads to transformation or lasting change. Without creating an authentic *purpose* that guides us and helps make us a community, without a *vision* of where we are going and how to get there, without inviting *ownership* and infusing the vision into the larger culture, and without the commitment to serve one another in the pursuit of a common vision, building capacity only through information or work meetings has little impact. Each of these pillars is an important context for the other. This combined, integrated context creates the conditions for change. In many ways this process is also emergent.

We feel that the ideas of emergent teaching can be a productive, if not an essential part of project-based learning, PLCs, and other student-oriented innovations. Emergent teaching is both a focus and a process. It is a way of thinking, but more importantly a way of seeing and being in the world. As this occurs, natural transformations result.

Emergent teaching comes to life when incorporated into a parallel meta-curriculum that pervades the whole school culture. This book can be used as a catalyst to share your stories and work toward an emerging vision of your own. It provides the conditions and understandings for emergent change—or change from within. When a person or group enters the "space of emergence" the multithreaded tales of our experience are both created and shared. And the process begins, only to be iterated over and over again.

It is our hope that this book will be useful as a guide to our readers' own meandering journeys of emergence and transformation. We would love to hear your questions, insights, frustrations, and successes. Consider contacting us at the information contained in the back of this book. May your journey inspire others and affect the lives of your students in the most positive ways.

Epilogue

This book has been a journey for us. As we stated in the introduction, the book came out of an ongoing conversation that spanned several years. Most of our conversations took place outside of educational institutions; we have found that emergent thinking flourishes in settings where there is no institutionalized agenda or single focus. We recommend getting away from the workplace whenever possible. It helps in terms of relaxing into a more open and expanded mode of thinking and in cultivating more meaningful relationships with colleagues.

Our conversations meandered to unfamiliar and sometimes exotic territory as we uncovered ideas and methodologies that at first seemed incompatible but eventually made sense. In this way our trust and familiarity with the dynamics of emergence grew.

Our conversations were laden with stories. These stories became gifts as we began to understand them as sources for natural inquiry. They came out of the mythos of the classroom but were also bound up within our own personal histories. They became emergent narratives that embedded much of what we sought to understand.

Our hope is that these stories and conversations will continue far beyond this book and the two of us. We want to encourage readers both in and out of the classroom to share and explore your own stories and narratives. After all, what you do with this book is what matters and what will have lasting impact.

Our friendship grew out of a shared passion for education and a mutual desire to see it change in ways that embrace values such as creativity, passion, and altruism. Because we come from different backgrounds (one of us is trained in academia, the other as an artist) it doesn't mean we are limited to these definitions. In the spirit of emergence, we believe the creative energy that comes out of the synthesis of these two sensibilities informs the writing in ways that give it added substance and meaning.

We are teachers, but again neither of us feels hostage to our chosen discipline; rather we see teaching as an emerging vocation that insists we transcend limiting identities. Both our teaching and our conversations are an exchange. We have tried to make the language and ideas accessible but also challenging. Our intention is that you, the reader, will feel encouraged to discover your own field of emergence, not just in the classroom but in all that you do. This is not a philosophy of education, but a "way" (in the spiritual sense) of developing an awareness of an event-centric world in which perceiving and acting form a single unity.

It is our students who have embraced these values, who have been courageous and unremitting in their pursuit of meaning, and this in spite of the enormous pressures from an educational system to narrow the scope of inquiry and conform to its way of framing knowledge. One high school teacher who was part of our graduate program said recently, "The more we think we know, the less we learn. When we know that we do not know, we are open to the wonders of the universe."

May you too step into this "space of emergence." We hope this book assists you in creating a vision where you realize that transformation and possibility are natural to who you are.

References

Abram, D. (1997). *The spell of the sensuous.* New York: Vintage Books.

Ames, R., Hall, D., and Lao Zi. (2003). *Dao de jing: A philosophical translation.* New York: Ballantine Books.

Applebee, A. (1996). *Curriculum as conversation: Transforming traditions of teaching and learning.* Chicago: University of Chicago Press.

Ashton, W., and Denton, D. (Eds.). (2006). *Spirituality, ethnography, and teaching: Stories from within.* New York: Peter Lang.

Baleskar, R. (2007). *The only way to live.* Mumbai, India: Yogi Impressions Books.

Berger, J. (1977). *Ways of seeing.* London: Penguin Books.

Berman, M. (1981). *The reenchantment of the world.* Ithaca, NY: Cornell University Press.

Biesta, G., and Osberg, D. (2010). Complexity, education and politics from the inside-out and the outside-in. In D. Osberg and G. Biesta (Eds.), *Complexity theory and the politics of education* (1–4). Rotterdam: Sense Publications.

Bloom, B. (1984). *Taxonomy of educational objectives.* Boston: Addison-Wesley.

Bohm, D., and Peat, D. (1997). Science, order, and creativity. London: Routledge.

Boran, S., and Comber, B. (2001). *Critiquing whole language and classroom inquiry.* Urbana, IL: National Council of Teachers of English.

Borges, J. L. (1967). *Jorge Luis Borges: A personal anthology.* A. Kerrigan (Ed.). New York: Grove Books.

Bruner, J. (2006). *Actual minds, possible worlds.* Boston: Harvard University Press.

Buhner, S. (2004). *The secret teachings of plants: The intelligence of the heart in the direct perception of nature.* Rochester, VT: Bear and Company.

Caine, G., Caine, R., and Crowell, S. (1999). *Mindshifts: A brain compatible process for professional development and the renewal of education.* Tucson, AZ: Zephyr Press.

Caine, R., and Caine, G. (1991). *Making connections: Teaching and the human brain.* Alexandria, VA: ASCD.

Caine, R., and Caine, G. (2011). *Natural learning for a connected world: Education, technology, and the human brain.* New York: Teachers College Press.

Caine, R., Caine, G., McClintic, C., Klimek, K. (2009). *12 brain/mind learning principles in action: Developing executive functions of the human brain.* Thousand Oaks, CA: Corwin Press.

Capra, F. (1997). *The web of life: A new scientific understanding of living systems.* New York: Anchor Books.

Childre, D., Martin, H., and Beech, D. (2000). *The heartmath solution.* New York: HarperCollins Publishers.

Clark, E. (2002). *Designing and implementing an integrated curriculum.* Brandon, VT: Holistic Education Press.

Claxton, G. (1997). *Hare brain, tortoise mind.* London: The Ecco Press.

Cloninger, R. (2004). *Feeling good: The science of well-being.* Oxford: Oxford University Press.

Cobb, J. (2003). *Process perspective: Frequently asked questions about process theology.* New York: Chalice Press.

Collister, R. (2010). *A journey in search of wholeness and meaning.* Bern, Switzerland: Peter Lang.

Cozolino, L. (2008). *The healthy aging brain: Sustaining attachment, attaining wisdom.* New York: Norton.

Cozolino, L. (2010). *The neuroscience of psychotherapy: Healing the social brain.* New York: Norton.

Crowell, S. (1989). A new way of thinking: The challenge of the future. *Educational Leadership, 47(1),* 59–61.

Crowell, S. (1995). Landscapes of change: Toward a new paradigm for education. In B. Blair and R. Caine (Eds.), *Integrative learning as a pathway to teaching holism, complexity, and interconnectedness.* Lewiston, NY: Edwin Mellon Press.

Crowell, S., and Caine, R. (1997). Restructuring as an integrative process. In T. Jennings (Ed.), *Restructuring for integrative education.* Westpoint, CT: Bergin & Garvey.

Crowell, S., Caine, R., and Caine, G. (2001). *The re-enchantment of learning: A manual for teacher renewal and classroom transformation.* Thousand Oaks, CA: Corwin Press.

Damasio, A. (1999). *The feeling of what happens: Body and emotion in the making of consciousness.* New York: Harvest Book, Harcourt.

Davies, P. (1983). *God and the new physics.* New York: Simon and Schuster.

Davis, B., and Sumara, D. (2006). *Complexity and education: Inquiries into learning, teaching, and research.* Mahwah, NJ: Lawrence Erlbaum.

Davis, B., Sumara, D., and Iftody, T. (2010). Complexity consciousness and curriculum. In D. Osberg and G. Biesta (Eds.), *Complexity theory and the politics of education* (107–120). Rotterdam: Sense Publications.

Davis, B., Sumara, D., and Luce-Kapler, R. (2000). *Engaging minds: Learning and teaching in a complex world.* Mahwah, NJ: Lawrence Erlbaum.

Diamond, M., and Hopson, J. (1999). *Magic trees of the mind: How to nurture your child's intelligence, creativity, and healthy emotions from birth through adolescence.* New York: Plume.

Doidge, D. (2007). *The brain that changes itself.* New York: Penguin.

Doll, W. (1993). *A post-modern perspective on curriculum.* New York: Teachers College Press.

Doll, W. (2005). The culture of method. In W. Doll, M. J. Fleener, D. Trueit, and J. St. Julien (Eds.), *Chaos, complexity, curriculum, and culture.* New York: Peter Lang.

Evans, M. (1998). *Whitehead and philosophy of education: The seamless coat of learning.* Amsterdam: Rodopi.

Evanshen, P., and Faulk, J. (2011). *A room to learn: Rethinking classroom environments.* New York: Gryphon House.

Fleener, M. J. (2005). Chaos, complexity, curriculum, and culture: Setting up the conversation. In W. Doll, M. J. Fleener, D. Trueit, and J. St. Julien (Eds.), *Chaos, complexity, curriculum and culture.* New York: Peter Lang.

Freire, P. (1970). *Pedagogy of the oppressed.* New York: Continuum.

Fuster, J. (2008). *The prefrontal cortex: The anatomy, physiology, and neuropsychology of the frontal lobe.* New York: Lippincott-Raven.

Gablik, S. (2002). *The reenchantment of art.* London: Thames and Hudson.

Gardner, H. (2007). *Five minds for the future.* Boston: Harvard Business Press.

Glassman, B. (2003). *Infinite circle: Teachings in Zen.* Boston: Shambhala Publications.

Glazer, S. (Ed.). (1999). *The heart of learning: Spirituality in education.* New York: Jeremy P. Tarcher/Putnam.

Goerner, S. J. (2001). *After the clockwork universe: The emerging science and culture of integral society.* Edinburgh: Floris Books.

Greene, M. (1988). *The dialectic of freedom.* New York: Teachers College Press.

Griffin, D. R. (1988). *The reenchantment of science.* Albany, NY: SUNY Press.

Hadot, P. (2005). *What is ancient philosophy?* (M. Chase, Trans.). Chicago: University of Chicago Press.

Hart, T. (2011). Supporting inner wisdom in public schools. In A. Johnson and M. Neagley (Eds.), *Educating from the heart: Theoretical and practical approaches to transforming education.* (13–24). Lanham, MD: Rowman & Littlefield.

Holman, P. (2011). *Engaging emergence: Turning upheaval into opportunity.* San Francisco: Berrett-Koehler.

Hyde, L. (2010). *Trickster makes this world: Mischief, myth, and art.* New York: Farrar, Straus, Giroux.

Jensen, E. (2007). *Introduction to brain-compatible learning.* Thousand Oaks, CA: Corwin Press.

Johnson, A. (2011). Developing spirit-related capacities of children and adolescents. In A. Johnson and M. Neagley (Eds.), *Educating from the heart: Theoretical and practical approaches to transforming education.* (3–2). Lanham, MD: Rowman & Littlefield.

Johnson, S. (2001). *Emergence: The connected lives of ants, brains, cities, and software.* New York: Simon and Schuster.

Kirshenblatt-Gimblett, B. (1998). *Destination culture: Tourism, museums, and heritage.* Berkeley, CA: University of California Press.

Kittay, E. (1987). *Metaphor: Its cognitive force and linguistic structure.* Oxford: Oxford University Press.

Klimak, K., Ritzenhein, E., and Sullivan, K. (2008). *Generative leadership: Shaping new futures for today's schools.* Thousand Oaks, CA: Corwin Press.

Lanza, R. (2009). *Biocentrism: How life and consciousness are the keys to understanding the true nature of the universe.* Dallas: BenBella Books.

Larrivee, B. (2008). *Authentic classroom management: Creating a learning community and building reflective practice.* New York: Pearson.

Laszlo, E. (1996). *The whispering pond: A personal guide to the emerging vision of science.* Rockport, MA: Element.

Lehrer, J. (2012). *Imagine: How creativity works.* New York: Houghton, Mifflin, Harcourt.

Lipton, B. (2005). *The biology of belief.* Santa Rosa, CA: Elite Books.

Louv, R. (2012). *The nature principle: Reconnecting with life in a virtual age.* New York: Workman Publishing.

Meadows, D. (2008). *Thinking in systems: A primer.* D. Wright (Ed.). White River Junction, VT: Chelsea Green Publishing.

Medina, J. (2009). *Brain rules: Twelve principles for surviving and thriving at work, home, and school.* Seattle: Pear Press.

Miller, J. P. (2001). *The holistic curriculum.* Toronto: OISE Press.

Miller, J. P. (2010). *Whole child education.* Toronto: University of Toronto Press.

Moore, T. (1992). *In care of the soul.* New York: HarperCollins.

Nadeau, R., and Kafatos, M. (2001). *The non-local universe: The new physics and matters of the mind.* Oxford: Oxford University Press.

Needleman, J. (1986). *The heart of philosophy.* New York: Jeremy P. Tarcher/Penguin.

Nelson, C. (2011). *I simply teach.* Yucca Valley, CA: Xlibris.

Oliver, D. (1989). *Education, modernity, and fractured meaning: Toward a process theory of teaching and learning.* Albany, NY: SUNY Press.

Osberg, D. (2010). Taking care of the future: The complex responsibility of education and politics. In D. Osberg and G. Biesta (eds). *Complexity theory and the politics of education.* Rotterdam: Sense Publishers.

Osberg, D., and G. Biesta (eds). (2008). *Complexity theory and the politics of education.* Rotterdam: Sense Publishers.

O'Sullivan, E. (1999). *Transformative Learning: Educational vision for the 21st century.* London: Zed Books.

Pausch, R. (2008). *The last lecture.* New York: Hyperion.

Percy, W. (1959). *The message in the bottle.* New York: Farrar, Straus, and Giroux.

Pinar, W. (2008). *What is curriculum theory?* New York: Taylor and Francis.

Pink, D. (2006). *A whole new mind: Why right-brainers will rule the future.* New York: Riverhead Books.

Plotkin, B. (2007). *Nature and the human soul: Cultivating wholeness and community in a fragmented world.* Novato, CA: New World Library.

Prigogine, I., and Stengers, I. (1984). *Order out of chaos: Man's new dialogue with nature.* New York: Bantam Books.

Ramachandran, V. S. (2011). *The tell-tale brain: A neuroscientist's quests for what makes us human.* New York: Norton.

Ramo, J. (2009). *The age of the unthinkable: Why the new world disorder constantly surprises us and what we can do about it.* New York: Little, Brown.

Rasmussen, J. (2010). Increasing complexity by reducing complexity. In D. Osberg and G. Biesta (Eds.), *Complexity theory and the politics of education* (15–24). Rotterdam: Sense Publishers.

Rendon, L. (2009). *Sentipensante pedagogy: Educating for wholeness, social justice, and liberation.* Sterling, VA: Stylus Publishing.

Rilke, Rainer Maria (1903). Letter four. http://en.wikiquote.org/wiki/Rainer_Maria_Rilke.

Robinson, K. (2011). *Out of our minds: Learning to be creative.* West Sussex, UK: Capstone/Wiley.

Roizen, M., and Oz, M. (2008). *You being beautiful: The owner's manual to inner and outer beauty.* New York: Free Press.

Samaras, A., Freese, A., Kosnic, C., and Beck, C. (2008). *Learning communities in practice.* Dordrecht: Springer Academic.

Sapolsky, R. (2004). *Why zebras don't get ulcers.* New York: Holt.

Sawyer, K. (2012). *Explaining creativity: The science of human innovation.* Oxford: Oxford University Press.

Schiering, M., Bogner, D., and Buli-Holmberg, J. (2011). *Teaching and learning: A model for academic and social cognition.* Lanham, MD: Rowman & Littlefield.

Schlemmer, P., and Schlemmer, D. (2008). *Teaching beyond the test: Differentiated project-based learning in a standards-based age.* Minneapolis, MN: Free Press.

Schwahn, C., and Spady, W. (2002). *Total leaders: Applying the best future-focused change strategies to education.* Lanham, MD: Rowman & Littlefield.

Schwartz, J., and Begley, S. (2002). *The mind and the brain: Neuroplasticity and the power of mental force.* New York: Regan Books.

Seed, J., Macy, J., and Fleming, P. (2007). *Thinking like a mountain: Towards a council of all beings.* Philadelphia: New Society Publishers.

Seligmann, A., Weller, R. P., Puett, M., and Simon, B. (2008). *Ritual and its consequences: An essay on the limits of sincerity.* Oxford: Oxford Press.

Shapiro, E. (2010). *Academic skills problems.* New York: Guilford Press.

Siegel, D. (1999). *The developing mind: How relationships and the brain interact to shape who we are.* New York: Guilford Press.

Smitherman, S. (2005). Chaos and complexity theories: Wholes and holes in curriculum. In W. Doll, M. J. Fleener, D. Trueit, and J. St. Julien (Eds.), *Chaos, complexity, curriculum and culture.* New York: Peter Lang.

Spring, J. (2007). *Wheels in the head: Educational philosophies of authority, freedom and culture: From Confucianism to human rights.* New York: McGraw-Hill.

Steinberg, L. (2010). *Adolescence.* New York: McGraw-Hill.

Stoddard, L. (2010). *Educating for human greatness.* Sarasota FL: Peppertree Press.

Stivers, E. (1990). *Metaphor: Forms and functions in qualitative research—nine case studies.* Presented at the American Educational Research Conference.

Swimme, B. (2002). *The hidden heart of the cosmos: Humanity and the new story.* Maryknoll, NY: Orbis Books.

Swimme, B., and Tucker, E. (2011). *Journey of the universe.* Hartford, CT: Yale University Press.

Taubman, S. (2005). *Unhypnosis: How to wake up, start over, and create the life you're meant to live.* Williston VT: Powertrack Publications.

Thompson, E. (2007). *Mind in life: Biology, phenomenology, and the sciences of mind.* London: Belknap Press of Harvard University Press.

Toulmin, S. (1982). *The return to cosmology: Post-modern science and the theology of nature.* Berkeley: University of California Press.

Varela, F., Thompson, E., and Rosch, E. (1993). *The embodied mind: Cognitive science and human experience.* Boston: MIT Press.

Vygotsky, L. S. (1978). *Mind in society: The development of higher psychological processes.* Boston: Harvard University Press.

Wertsch, J. (1998). *Mind in action.* Oxford: Oxford Press.

Whitehead, A. N. (1967). *The aims of education.* New York: Free Press.

Wilson, R. (2007). *Nature and young children: Encouraging creative play and learning in natural environments.* New York: Routledge.

Wink, J. (2010). *Critical pedagogy: Notes from the real world.* New York: Pearson.

Zull, J. (2002). *The art of changing the brain: Enriching the practice of teaching by exploring the biology of learning.* Sterling, VA: Stylus Publishers.

Zull, J. (2011). *From brain to mind: Using neuroscience to guide change in education.* Sterling, VA: Stylus Publishers.

Index

About the Authors

Sam Crowell is professor of education at California State University, San Bernardino, and founder and codirector of the MA in Holistic and Integrative Education. The program has been recognized nationally as a model of transformative learning in a study funded by the Fetzer Foundation and published in the *Journal for Transformative Education*, and it has produced five educators who have been recognized as teacher-of-the-year.

David Reid-Marr is adjunct professor in the MA in Holistic and Integrative Education at California State University, San Bernardino, and teaches full time at the Idyllwild Arts Academy, a highly regarded high school for the arts.